D1300266

BUILD TO LAUGH:
How To Construct
Sketch Comedy With
The Fast and Funny Formula

By Cherie Kerr

© Copyright 1996 by Cherie Kerr

All rights reserved. No part of this book may be reproduced or utilized
in any form or by any means, electronic or mechanical, including
photocopying, recording or by any information storage and retrieval system,
without permission in writing from the Publisher. Inquires should be
addressed to
ExecuProv Press
809 North Main Street
Santa Ana, CA 92701

ExecuProv Press

Printed in the United States of America

ISBN #0-9648882-2-X

FOR Heather

you moko-face

Acknowledgements

There are so many to whom I owe a debt of gratitude for guiding me as a writer; others for guiding me as a person. They include: Joe Martin, Mary Bennett, Jan Kaye, and Skip Pedigo for believing in me early on; Gary Austin for his never-ending influence; Tom Maxwell for his encouragement; Bud for teaching me that mediocre isn't good enough; Dr. Peggy and Linda; Mama Patsy and Greg for all their kind words; Gus for his cheerleading; Audrey for keeping me on course; Alex for making me take chances; Shannon and Drake for nudging me every step of the way; Judy, my rock; my father for just being my father; and my mother — she dances with the light, now.

A Very Special Thanks To:

Vivian, Alan, Mich and Nina

Table of Contents

INTRODUCTION

Maybe it's the difficult times we live in — life is fast paced; technology is replacing the human connection; and we're faced with serious concerns about the environment, personal safety, values, the American Dream — but it seems now more than ever we're in need of humor and laughter as antidotes to all that intensity.

Humor provides relief. Humor helps us depersonalize. It defuses anger and neutralizes resentment. Humor gives us a healthier perspective. It enables us to make sense of the ridiculous, and to bear up under tragedy. All in all, humor makes us feel better; it's that simple.

In recent years, the use of humor as a staple in various forms of entertainment— on stage and screen— has steadily increased. We've seen the expansion of comedy clubs throughout the country, and the proliferation of humor-oriented programming on television, including sitcoms and even knock-offs of the long-running *Saturday Night Live*. And now there's a cable channel devoted entirely to providing comedy of all types, 24 hours a day. The advent of additional cable channels and the widespread use of the Internet will undoubtedly heighten the demand for comedy as entertainment. Like I said, the times we live in beg for more laughter.

As outlets and demands for comedy grow, there'll be a corresponding need for all forms of humorous material, and for the writers who create it. Within that arena of supply and demand lies sketch comedy— one of the most enjoyable and therapeutically beneficial types of comedy around.

The writing of sketch comedy is an art unto itself. While humorous ideas are plentiful, making them work in the sketch comedy format is hard to do. Since sketches are of relatively short duration, they must be concise and entertaining at the same time. Fortunately for aspiring sketch comedy writers, there's more method than madness to building solid comedy pieces.

Build To Laugh: How To Construct Sketch Comedy With The Fast and Funny Formula is designed to help any writer who wants to turn out workable, consistently good, sketch comedy material with every attempt. And I'm not referring solely to comedy writers, either. I'm also talking about people who want to write a funny sketch for an annual company event; theater students who want to explore sketch comedy as a possible career choice; and anyone else with an interest, good ideas, and maybe even some fragments of clever dialogue, but in need of an appropriate format for showcasing his or her talents.

All of these individuals face the same dilemma: the "how" of crafting sketch comedy — how to go from a great idea, through the sketch, to a knock-'em-dead ending. Well, this book provides an answer to that dilemma.

Build To Laugh first defines for you the nature of sketch comedy, the prerequisites of preparation for writing it, and your unique style in presenting it. Then it'll proceed carefully through each of the eight steps of the "Fast and Funny Formula" for writing sketch comedy, with plenty of examples and exercises along the way for you to try. In fact, the bulk of this book is a nuts-and-bolts discussion of how to assemble sketch comedy. Additional sections are devoted to working the "Fast and Funny Formula," and the introduction of writing particulars, such as writing alone vs. collaborating with others. There's even a worksheet to help you write out your own sketches using the eight steps of the formula.

This book is also dedicated to helping you, the writer, discover your unique strengths, point of view, and frame of reference. Further, it's meant to open up channels of creativity you weren't even aware existed, so you'll have increased access to original, humorous ideas. Occasional chapter assignments will encourage you to test your writing capabilities. Additionally, a sampling of full-length sketches will be broken down step by step to clearly illustrate for you why these particular comedy pieces succeeded— or failed to succeed— on stage.

In the nearly 30 years I've been involved in comedy, I've observed, analyzed, and written literally hundreds of sketches. I've also taught and coached dozens of writers, and story-edited comedy pieces that were ill-crafted and faltering. In the process, I've gotten very familiar— sometimes painfully so— with what does and doesn't work in sketch comedy.

As a result of my experiences, I've agonized over how to offer a formula and guidelines that will be helpful to beginning sketch comedy writers. So it's in that spirit, and with that intent, I offer the following chapters to you.

Understanding Sketch Comedy, You, and the Connection Between the Two

What Is Sketch Comedy?

The Many Different Types of Comedy

Comedy is like ice cream: it comes in an assortment of flavors, including stand-up, improv, sitcoms, plays, screenplays, Broadway musicals, burlesque, skits and sketches. While all comedy is essentially the same "food," each type has a slightly different taste to it. For example, stand-up comedy is usually a compilation of short build-ups with the promise of a one-line punchline, while improv is "in the moment" and created as it's spoken. Sitcoms combine an A, B, C complexity of plots, characters, and themes— all of which are magically tied together by the end of the episode. Comedic plays and screenplays are full-length accounts of characters, events, and stories; Broadway musicals are sung in and around their stories and humor. Burlesque, the early antecedent to most forms of comedy today, features a broad array of humorous bits and pieces.

While skits or sketches are closely related to the burlesque tradition, they can feature all of the above comedy forms in a condensed or reduced version, which is what makes writing them so much fun. Sketch comedy covers a broad base, and the limits are few.

Sketch Comedy and Satire

Sketch comedy is almost always satirical. Tom Maxwell,

Artistic Director of the L.A. Groundlings for 13 years, says that satire is meant to either denigrate or exaggerate. I advise my own students that to make satire is to make fun of. As you can imagine, there are many, many ways to do this. Just look around you. The fact is, we can make fun of just about anything or anyone, especially ourselves.

A satirical piece should always make a statement or a point; quite often it has a "bite" to it, which can be a healthy way of criticizing people or things. While I personally hate to see satire taken to the extreme in a malicious way, I think if done tastefully, it can send a powerful message without being offensive or alienating.

Now, if you're hypersensitive, satire can sometimes seem mean or cruel; but if you have a well-developed sense of humor, it's a great way to make yourself and others laugh at the imperfections of an imperfect world. In fact, writing about those imperfections can be a great catharsis. I know in my own case, people and things I'm upset about often end up on my stage; and I consider myself fortunate to be able to vent my frustrations through my shows -- the best, most constructive therapy I can imagine.

Sketch Comedy – The Formula

The formula for writing sketch comedy will be covered in great detail in the following chapters, but let me give you a preview of what's involved.

In the course of completing the eight steps of the "Fast and Funny Formula," you'll identify your idea and its category, and pinpoint what's funny about it and where the joke is. You'll also make decisions as to your point of view/frame of reference and the concept or premise of your piece. The first four steps will serve as the blueprint for building your comedy sketch. In the remaining four steps of the process you'll do the actual construction of the piece, including the outside structure, the inside structure or beats, the filler (the dialogue and activities of your characters), and last— but definitely not least— the ending. And by the time you complete the formula, you'll feel very comfortable with all these new terms.

Classic Comedy Sketches

There are lots of great sketches and sketch characters to review for inspiration. How about *"Laugh-In's"* Arte Johnson as the dirty old man who was always trying to pick up Ruth Buzzi, or Lily Tomlin's "Edith Ann" and "Ernestine?" Or pieces from *"Saturday Night Live"* like "Those Wild and Crazy Guys," "The Blues Brothers," Bill Murray's "Lounge Lizard," Gilda Radner's "Baba WaaWaa," Dana Carvey's "Church Lady," and Jon Lovitz's "Tommy Flannigan?" Then there's Carol Burnett's "Washer Woman" and her portrayal of Scarlett O'Hara; and from *"In Living Color,"* "Varicosa," "Wanda," and "Homey the Clown."

The above sketches were all built around characters, but sketch comedy is just as likely to revolve around things. *"Saturday Night Live,"* for instance, has made jokes about everything from guns in schools to breakfast cereals, while *"In Living Color"* has bashed infomercials and lifestyles of the homeless. Renowned improv groups like The Second City and the L.A. Groundlings (and my own group, The Orange County Crazies) have made sport of any and all current events, lifestyles, trends, and attitudes.

There's really no limit as to what you can target in sketch comedy. The goal is to be original and inventive; and I think each writer possesses a point of view that's unique and slightly off-center from everyone else's. And that brings me to my closing point: you can write on the same subject in a zillion different ways.

What Makes People Laugh?

Laughing is for Everyone

Everyone laughs at something. We laugh at what's absurd, tragic, exaggerated, frustrating, stupid. Very often we laugh at the truth.

Researchers have conducted many studies in the past few years to discover why people laugh. Patricia Keith-Spiegel, a psychologist, offers the following eight theories about possible sources of laughter:

◆ Surprise — The unexpected tickles us

◆ Superiority — We need to equalize with those "above" us or put down those "below" us

◆ Biological — A born and bred instinct

◆ Incongruity — Clashing of ideas and perceptions

◆ Ambivalence — The stresses of conflicting emotions

◆ Release — An effort to unlock life's tensions and inhibitions

◆ Configurational — Sudden insight from having solved a problem

◆ Psychoanalytical — Like sleep, it's therapeutic

As you're searching for ideas and sources of humor for constructing your comedy pieces, keep these theories in mind; they can help guide you in the right direction. And with a small degree of self-examination, I'm sure you'll be able to find loads of material in your own life that corresponds to each of the eight theories.

Other research studies have focused on sense of humor, including what constitutes it; where we get it; why some people are more likely than others to use it as a communication tool; and why it's so vital to each of us. In his book, *Comedy Writing Step by Step*, Gene Perret devotes several pages to a definition of the term. He suggests in order to have and maintain a sense of humor, we need the following abilities:

◆ The ability to see things as they are
◆ The ability to recognize things as they are
◆ The ability to accept things as they are.

[In addition, he states that humor tends to reassure the insecure, is the weapon of the underdog, and serves as social criticism — more grist for the writing mill.]

I believe everyone's born with a sense of humor; it's a God-given gift. How that gift is developed, nurtured, and utilized depends on the individual. Comedy writers, in particular, get to play with their senses of humor day in and day out; that's why I think they're some of the luckiest people on the planet.

A sense of humor allows us to cope with the worst of our personal tragedies; and our tragedies, in turn, often provide us with a very rich source of humor. (Unfortunately, it sometimes takes us years to spot the funnier aspects of our "tragedy"!) I know my own sense of humor has virtually saved my life at various low points.

Humor is bonding and endearing. Humor is positive energy. Humor is, above all, one of the healthiest outlets for our minds and bodies. And humor is like a muscle: if you use it constantly, it'll stay toned, flexible, agile, and strong.

Looking in the Laughing Mirror

I always advise my students to take careful note of what makes them laugh. It seems that each of us — whether due to our upbringing or the culmination of life experiences — tends to laugh harder at some things more than others. Some people react heartily to the Laurel and Hardy brand of comedy, but not to the more intellectual offerings of a Dennis Miller. Some laugh readily when the joke's at another person's expense, while others are more likely to get a kick out of their own faux paux and shortcomings. A pie in the face may be funnier than a Marx Brothers' quip, a "Bassomatic" demonstration more hilarious than a bowl of "Colon Blow," and an attempt by Lucy to stomp grapes more hilarious than a "shot to the moon" by Jackie Gleason. Or maybe it's a one-line retort by George Burns that tickles us in our deepest funny parts, or perhaps the wry topical recaps of Jay Leno vs. the Top Ten lists of David Letterman.

No matter what type of humor gets you laughing, be sure to make note of it. Once you're clear on that point, you can begin the preparation process for creating your very own sketch material. So let me remind you: Look closely, look carefully, and look often at what makes you laugh.

Preparation for Writing Sketch Comedy

Getting Ready

Before beginning the sketch writing process, you must carefully scrutinize what makes you laugh. You'll write better material if it comes from the core of your funny bone rather than the vantage point of what other writers find humorous. With wit and a variety of life experiences at your disposal, you should have enough material for a lifetime's worth of writing.

Take a Look at Then and Now

Everyone's childhood is a potential gold mine for jokes, even though it doesn't always seem that way. We laugh at Bill Cosby's account of his upbringing, as well as at Louie Anderson's. Why not ours? The perceptions of young people are always comedic; and every one of us had some fairly bizarre points of view, fears, likes and dislikes, and needs while growing up. Plus, no two childhoods are the same.

And what about your adult life thus far? Note your passages and growth patterns. Each chunk of living tends to have its funny stuff. A bitter divorce, for example, may not seem funny when you're going through it, but years later might be a source of humor. Remember: the more experience — and the more profound it is — the more material you'll have available to you. That's why I feel strongly that the best comedy writers are people in their 40s, 50s, and 60s.

And, of course, you can always look to the everyday happenings around you for potential writing material. The topical issues, the people in the news, the trends, the attitudes, the changing mores. People you like. People you hate. I think creating sketches is easier to do if you write about present things and current people; there's so much to choose from and so much that strikes a common chord with the audience.

Again, though, it goes back to what strikes *you* as funny — what makes, or has made, a strong impression on you. So look to the past, the present, and definitely to the absurdity of trying to predict or envision the future.

Look At Why They're Laughing

After you examine your own sense of humor, start taking a look at the people close to you to figure out what makes them laugh. Are they laughing harder than you are at certain things? Can you identify some universal funny spots you think all of us have? Are there consistent similarities among certain stories, movies and jokes; that is, is everyone laughing at the same time, in the same way?

As a comedy writer-to-be, you'll need to investigate for yourself what makes an audience laugh. (Don't forget: we're all audience members, too, at one time or another.) You'll probably find, as I have, that some audiences are more responsive than others. Most of the time, though, audiences will laugh at the same spots, at the same lines, throughout.

Knowing what makes other people laugh will help to broaden your awareness when writing. So even if your sense of humor pleases you, take note of what pleases others. In fact, learning to be more objective than subjective when it comes to humor may be one of the most valuable comedy lessons of all.

So, by analyzing your own sense of humor first, and then assimilating other people's humor perceptions, you'll have a much better understanding of why people laugh. And after the understanding comes the writing. Funny writing. Now's the time to put up your antennae and take in as much as you can. Believe me, it'll make all the difference in producing writing that's consistently funny -- comedy hits rather than comedy misses.

Take a Laughter Field Trip

Visit a comedy club, see a movie at a theater (not on your VCR), take in an improv performance, sit through several showings of a theme park comedy performance, attend an open rehearsal for a comedy play, go to a comedy class. There are endless opportunities and a variety of venues for observing people's reactions to comedy. I've coached quite a few actors and writers, and I always tell both types the same thing: A good actor is a good observer.

Keep a Log

As my students begin preparation for the sketch-writing process, I instruct them to keep a small notebook with them at all times and tuck it away where it's easy to get to. You never know when something you see, or do, will trigger an idea for a sketch. Ideas are so fleeting sometimes that unless you've written them down, you'll be unable to retrieve them when you really need to. You've probably heard people say — or said it yourself — "I had this great idea, but now I can't remember it. Oh, what was it?" For this reason, all the comedy writers I know have steno pads strapped to their chests and pens dangling from their wrists.

Think of it the same way as a sneeze and the need for Kleenex. So number one rule: Carry a pen and notepad at all times. Otherwise, you may be forced to jot down "your moment" on, well, something that's really handy like — a piece of Kleenex!

If you have a small laptop, that's great; but be sure to print out your notes soon after you've logged them. I prefer to have hard copies in hand of everything I take note of. There are simply too many sad stories about machinery that crashed, or computers that were taken. Now, who'd steal a notepad?

Make a List

Keep ideas, pieces of ideas, words, phrases, impressions, comments, and sensory information on a list inside your notebook. Many things you record today will also be good tomorrow (most things on my list have proved to be timeless). Even if you don't return to the list for quite a while — sometimes I leave things on mine for two or three years before completing them, and I know other writers who do the same — you'll have it when you need it. In fact, the list will probably be the origin of almost every sketch you write; and it's a great resource to tap into when your well of creativity is running low.

Don't Hold Back

When you're making entries on your list, try to avoid falling into the trap of thinking "What a dumb idea." Everything is worthy of being listed. Sometimes we buckle under our own pressure and censor our initial thoughts before they can develop into something concrete and workable. Don't dismiss a thought before you can even get it down on paper. Record it. Let go. A free mind is a creative mind. You don't want to get into the habit of unduly restricting yourself in the preliminary stages of sketch comedy writing. You can always discard ideas later. Build an arsenal. Believe me, you'll need it when you get ready to reload your mind and fire off those funny pieces.

Take A Time Out

Another strategy for preparing to write is to simply let your mind wander. Sit quietly and allow things to come to you. Put yourself in a place without any distractions. Make this a daily ritual. Many writers (including myself) do this at a specific time every day. Some call it meditation.

After a while, you may find yourself waking from sleep with a multitude of sketch writing possibilities — you know, those moments when you first awaken and lie in bed, quietly thinking. If you're not ready for them, the ideas may come at you too quickly to be written down; so be sure to take your notepad to bed with you.

Discover Yourself

When you spend enough time — quietly — inside your own head, you'll learn a great deal about your unique and very personalized sense of humor. This knowledge will have everything to do with the sketch writing approach you eventually adopt. So pay close attention to all discoveries of this kind (record them in your notebook); they'll help to guide you through the writing process. Think of them like bread crumbs scattered on the trail, leading you "home."

You're Almost Ready

I have to reiterate the importance of the preparation lesson. Not preparing would be the equivalent of running a marathon without first stretching your muscles. For this event, you must ready your mental muscles. Study what makes you and others laugh; record your thoughts; tap into your background and life experiences; and observe closely. If you prepare in this way, you'll be ready to launch yourself into the sketch-writing arena; and once there, you'll be able to truly and freely express yourself.

Your Comedy Writing Voice

After completing the preparation process discussed in the previous chapter, the next practical step is to identify your comedy voice. In comedy writing terms, "voice" refers to the way you state your material, your unique style of expression. Just like your speaking voice has a particular DNA sound imprint, your comedy voice captures your unique, individual slant on the material you've chosen. It's the sound of your voice, metaphorically speaking, that sets you apart from others in the writing field.

Look Closely For a Positive Identification

Finding your comedy voice is as simple as looking within to discover your unique way of expressing your thoughts and feelings. If you do that, you're sure to discover something specific and meaningful to say. And during the writing process, you'll need to be aware of your specific thoughts and feelings as they relate to the topic you've selected. (As you can see, comedy really is a very personal thing.)

For myself, there are some things I'm simply not interested in and/or not qualified to write about; but there are other topics I can write on endlessly. It took time for me to identify my comedy writing voice, so don't get discouraged if you can't immediately find yours. Enjoy the process. And once you do locate your writing voice, you'll discover it's got a place all its own; it doesn't sound like any other writer; and nothing you say will have been said quite that way before. I find when I'm true to my own voice — my niche, so to speak — I'm able to turn out critically acclaimed work.

It's Your Thing, So Do What You Want To Do

Write about what you know. Although I write on a broad array of topics, my comedy voice tends to be strongest when I'm writing biting satire about the contemporary adult female. I write about Yuppie issues. Middle America. Single motherhood. Having it all as an overachieving professional. Divorce. Child support. Equality in marriage. Material addictions and vanity obsessions. And many other subjects that are important to me. These areas strike a personal nerve; so when I write about them, the material comes from deep within. In fact, one critic from the *Los Angeles Times* claims he can always distinguish my comedy pieces in a show, because he's learned how to distinguish my creative "voice."

Now, how about you? What topics strike a chord? What issues do you feel most strongly about? It's important to identify them, because strong feelings and beliefs tend to generate the best sketch material.

Two Key Questions

Identifying your comedy voice will be easier if you can first establish your frame of reference and your point of view. Let me define those terms for you: "frame of reference" is your experience with a subject, how much you know about it; and "point of view" is your opinion or attitude with regard to that subject.

As you begin laying out the ideas and concepts for your comedy sketches (we'll get to that in Part Two), remember to keep asking yourself these two questions: "What is my frame of reference?" and "What is my point of view?" If you always write from the answers you get, your work will consistently speak in a particular way. Your way. Through your voice.

You And You Alone

In teaching sketch writing classes, it's been my experience that 99 percent of the time no two people will write exactly the same comedy piece, even if they start out with identical concepts or ideas. So out of 20 students, I'll get 20 different versions of the subject matter.

For example, I once asked a class of ten writers to provide concepts or premises from which they could write sketches about the fate of Prince Charles and/or Princess Diana. Here's what I got:

1. Prince Charles, it's revealed, likes to dress in the Queen's clothes, and finally "comes out" at a state dinner.

2. When Princess Diana files for divorce, she wants only the royal refrigerator (for food storage), and fights valiantly for it.

3. Princess Diana buys out Jenny Craig.

4. Prince Charles takes personality lessons from Danny DeVito.

5. Charles marries Fergie; Diana marries Andrew.

6. Charles goes from one dowdy woman to another — Camilla Parker Bowles to Janet Reno — and then settles down with Barbara Bush.

7. Diana opens her own publishing company and invites everyone she knows to write a memoir about her.

8. Free at last, Diana now goes on tour as a background dancer with Madonna.

9. Wills and Harry are seen conferring with Erik and Lyle Menendez.

10. Incognito, Diana stages a garage sale to augment her income, but when someone happens upon her wedding gown, the speculations start flying.

From one suggestion, then, my ten students came up with ten entirely different concepts, each having the potential to become a comedy sketch. How about you? What ideas could you quickly jot down on the same subject? Try to come up with five or six. As you do, examine your frame of reference and/or point of view with regard to the royal couple and their respective futures.

Put It All Together

As you go forward with the task of writing sketch comedy, see if you can discover, identify, and express your unique comedy voice. Keep asking yourself the two pertinent questions about point of view and frame of reference, and then carve a niche for yourself that gives you lots of space to roam, creatively speaking, and allows you to say things in ways that only you can say them.

1. Dodi & Diana didn't actually die in the tunnel in Paris but instead have been in hiding preparing to launch their own reality show, and procreating to rival Kate + 8.

2. Charles declares the Paris tunnel where Diana was killed a National Monument.

3. Diana joins forces with Courtney Love + Tori Spelling + creates a clothing line for anorexics

4. Diana launches a hair care system called "Older is Better" encouraging women to look older.

Writing to the Edge

Three Little Words

"I t's been done" — for a comedy writer, these are the three most dreaded words of all. It's painful, to say the least, to write an entire sketch only to be told that the idea, and your presentation of it, are not the wildly original creations you thought they were.

True, nothing is really original. In fact, the experts say that all art forms are simply recycled, revamped, or reconfigured versions of prior works. Certainly, this is true for sketch comedy. Look, for example, at the similarities between the work of: Carol Burnett and Lucille Ball; Robin Williams and Jonathan Winters; Laurel and Hardy, the Marx Brothers, and the Three Stooges. The concept for *"Saturday Night Live"* was borrowed from a show named *"That Was The Week That Was"*; in addition, SNL utilizes the character-driven approach popularized by the earlier *"Laugh- In."*

So, most of what we see in comedy is a compilation and restructuring of what's gone before. However, each time an idea is reinvented, it has the possibility of offering the audience an "edge" — an overused contemporary term for something new and different (as in "cutting edge technology," for example). In comedy writing, edge is where the humor is. If people use a phrase like "That was *so* funny when..." to describe a sketch, it usually means the comedy piece had a distinctive, memorable edge to it.

The Difference Between Edge and Voice

Now, edge shouldn't be confused with voice. Your comedy voice is your individual way of expressing an idea, based on personal experience or knowledge; it's the way you speak your piece or sketch. Edge, on the other hand, is what gives your idea something new — a spin, a twist, a jolt, a surprise, an original thrust, an addition to something's that's otherwise old; that's already been done.

And it's all very personal. Your edge, like your voice, is unlike any other writer's. It has a comedic imprint all its own, which you can demonstrate with each and every piece you create.

I think it's voice that provides the impetus to begin writing a sketch, and edge that supplies the inspiration. When you get a bizarre idea (edge) that fits comfortably within your premise (voice), you tend to be motivated to take it to the finish line, perhaps by weaving the "edge" through the sketch or punching the ending with it — however you do it. The end result: you'll please your audience.

Sketch With an Edge – An Example

In my improv group, the Orange County Crazies, we decided to do a parody of the famed *"Honeymooners"* television program. Obviously, this was something that'd been done many, many times before, so we needed an edge, or a spin, to make our version new and different. We found our inspiration in the everyday world of Orange County, which in the '80s and '90s has received a large influx of Asian-Americans, mostly Vietnamese.

We staged the skit in the familiar, dreary kitchen of the Kramden apartment, with three improv actors portraying the main characters, Alice, Ralph, and Norton. The actors imitated the vocal pitches and cadences, the facial expressions and mannerisms, and the personal characteristics we've come to associate with those three characters. The costumes, too, were replicas.

So what made our sketch different? What was our edge? Well, through the wonders of makeup, the actors looked Vietnamese; and they spoke Vietnamese — well, some approximation of it — throughout the entire sketch! Both the audience and the critics loved it. My group had brainstormed to find the "edge," and we'd succeeded.

Take It To the Edge and Jump

Hitting upon and developing the edge for a sketch is essential to its success. Edge is also one of the elements that marks a particular writer's style. Once someone views a piece and thinks to himself, "Oh, I bet so and so did that; it looks like something she'd write," that's quite an accomplishment. When that happens to you, you'll know you've made an impression on the sketch writing community — whether in a small town or Hollywood.

Once you've managed to present yourself in a clever way, on a consistent basis, you will have arrived. There's a high level of respect, and even awe, for a writer who's defined his voice and demonstrated edge. So, no matter what your mother told you, in this instance, *don't* look before you leap. Just go for it.

PART TWO

Getting Down To Business: Crafting Your Sketch

The Formula and Guidelines for Using It

The Formula

During my many years as a head writer and director of comedy sketches, I've encountered a number of actor/writers with great ideas, but no clue as to how to give those ideas form and substance. And because they weren't able to develop or write their concepts in a workable way, I had to sit by and watch with dismay as these potentially talented people fell squarely on their faces.

It gradually dawned on me that in order to bring their promising ideas to fruition, these would-be writers needed a framework and a set of guidelines for crafting sketch comedy. Just like dressmakers have patterns, cooks have recipes, and architects have blueprints, potential sketch writers needed a dot-to-dot process to get from A to Z — from the initial idea for a comedy piece to its successful, humorous conclusion. Ergo, the birth of the "Fast and Funny Formula," an eight-step sketch writing process you'll be learning in the following chapters.

This formula has been "scientifically" developed. I've tested it. I've worked and reworked it (at one point even throwing it away and starting again from scratch). To prove it works, I've retraced my own steps through the hundreds of comedy pieces I've written. Believe me, this formula does what it's supposed to do: provide a road map to aspiring comedy sketch writers so they can drive their comedy vehicles from one part of their minds to the next, reaching their destinations safely. And guess what? They can take the ride all by themselves, with no help from anyone else.

In devising the formula, I had other goals as well. I wanted to create something that was easy to follow and simple to implement. I wanted to make certain that anyone with good ideas and a creative mind could learn to do — in a relatively short period of time — what many writers take years to master. I wanted shortcuts and safety; humor and originality; and success for everyone who was willing to give the formula a try.

The lessons in Part Two are the heart of this book. They're meant to make a comedy sketch writer out of anyone who truly desires to learn the craft. One warning, though: the assignments must be carried out diligently and with dedication. And since no writer escapes paying his or her proverbial dues, you can expect to write and then rewrite your sketches before turning out a comedy piece that meets industry standards.

So my advice to you is: follow the directions given in the eight steps to come; persevere; enjoy the process. If you do, you're certain to be surprised and pleased with the final product — your comedy sketch.

Following The Guidelines – First Things First

As a comedy writer, I suggest you approach writing a sketch in much the same way an architect designs a house or a contractor builds it: step by step. The first thing you'll need, then, is a set of blueprints — the design and specifications for the comedy piece you're building. Once you have those, you can begin construction of your sketch from the ground up, making it solid and free-standing.

Before I introduce the procedure for crafting your comedy sketch, recall, if you will, the exercises you completed in Chapter 4, Part One, concerning preparation. Preparation is similar to the grading process that occurs before homebuilding gets underway. If your plot of land -- your mental space -- has been carefully graded or primed in advance, you should be ready to go. All that's required of you, then, is to follow your plans and begin construction. First, though, let me outline the eight steps that will take you from start to finish of the sketch-building process. The steps are:

Designing the Project (Blueprints)

1. Category
2. Purpose
3. Frame of reference or point of view
4. Concept or premise

Building The Project (Actual construction)

5. Outside structure (four principles to apply)
6. Inside structure — beats
7. Filler — dialogue and action
8. The Ending

By following each of these steps in order, you'll be able to progress from the origin of your sketch — your initial idea — to its actualization on stage. Along the way, keep reminding yourself that building a sketch is no different than building a house. And if, after completing the sketch, you decide you also want to direct it, you can then supply the final touches that'll really bring the sketch alive — just like adding furniture and landscaping to that newly finished home.

In addition, once you've learned how to go from start to finish of your comedy "house" using the eight-step formula, I'll be providing you with some supplemental terms and guidelines borrowed from the world of improv comedy. In fact, the "Fast and Funny Formula" is based on a method often used in developing and conducting improv scenes (many of which evolve into full-length, scripted sketches); so think of the improv rules and guidelines as valuable tools that'll assist you in the successful construction of *your* comedy piece.

And finally, just before leaving this section of the book, you'll find a chapter on writing for individual characters. Some comedy writers get so attached to this type of writing, they end up specializing in it. Maybe you will, too. The only way to find out is to give it a try.

Let's get started!

DESIGNING THE PROJECT (BLUEPRINTS)

Step 1: Category

Before drawing the blueprints for a comedy sketch, you must first understand what constitutes a solid foundation. The starting point here is selection of an appropriate category. If you can easily identify a category that triggers your desire to say something, then you've found a reasonable starting point. And while the number of possible categories is infinite, I recommend choosing one that stimulates self-examination. I've found that when my students look within at their thoughts and feelings, they often find something very definite they want to express.

Let's say, for example, you'd like to make a satirical statement about what's going on today on the political front. Great! You've successfully pinpointed a specific direction. Now, consider the following list of categories as a starting point for your sketch. (If you're still looking for that initial idea, begin by examining the categories and listing at least ten thoughts or feelings generated by your responses to them.)

The categories are:

1. What's topical
2. What bugs, scares, or intrigues you
3. What makes a strong impression on you (good or bad)

4. What pushes your emotional buttons
5. What's interesting about human nature
6. What you're obsessed with
7. What seems absurd
8. What your present (or past) secret thoughts or feelings are

As previously mentioned, the number of possible categories is infinite; but what I've listed above covers quite a broad range — perhaps wide enough to keep you writing for the rest of your life!

To add to the possibilities, you might also want to mix and match some of the categories in developing your comedy piece. For example, I once started with the category of a personal obsession: shoulder pads. (I wasn't alone in my preoccupation with wearing contoured lifts; in the early '90s, women all across the country were falling in love with them.) To me, this obsession seemed absurd; offered a fascinating glimpse into the workings of human nature; and was something I definitely had secret thoughts and feelings about. So although the initial idea for my sketch fell into the "something I'm obsessed with" category, it soon became apparent that I'd be drawing from other categories as well, which helped me to flesh out the piece as I continued to work on it.

(In fact, the "Too Much Shoulder Pad" sketch is presented in its entirety at the end of Chapter 8, and I'll be referring to it as we go along, to further explain each of the eight steps involved in sketch comedy construction.)

Step 2: Purpose

In the "Too Much Shoulder Pad" sketch, the selection of a category — "something I'm obsessed with" — gave me a direction for the piece. To move it along and justify my choice, though, I needed to ask myself two pertinent questions related to my purpose in writing the sketch: 1) "What's the point?"; and 2) "Where's the joke"? (The *point* is the reason for the satire; and the *joke* refers to what's funny about it.)

In justifying my reason for writing about shoulder pads, I'd observed that all the women I knew were suddenly feeling the need to wear them. The joke was that wearing shoulder pads had become addictive — so addictive, in fact, that women (me included) were attaching them to every single piece of clothing they owned. Plus, the pads themselves were steadily enlarging, becoming higher and wider at every turn. (Remember, satire often denigrates or exaggerates; in this case, exaggeration was the obvious byword.)

By answering the two questions with regard to point and joke, I now had a *purpose* for writing my piece. So I had progressed from having a primary category — personal obsession — to knowing the reason for talking about it and the source of its humor.

In general, when you know both the reason for saying something and where the joke is, everything else you lay out in the critical stages of planning will evolve easily and naturally. Unfortunately, I've seen many a would-be sketch writer show up at a writers' meeting with the fragment of an idea, but without a handle on the reason for talking about it and why it was funny; in other words, the idea lacked purpose. And when it came time for the writer to discuss the idea, it went nowhere. Let me give you a case in point.

A writer came to us with an idea he called "Hookers on Phonics," which was a great play on words and had the potential for being a good parody of the educational reading program, "Hooked on Phonics." However, when I asked the writer where he was going with the piece, he didn't know. After struggling to make that determination, he later collaborated with others to build an entire sketch around his initial idea. (Incidentally, the final piece was strong and very well received by the audience.)

In sum, having a "thing" about a particular topic strongly motivates you to want to talk about it; that, in turn, helps you identify the reason for discussing it and the joke(s) to be found there. Once again, the key to laying out a plan you'll return to again and again in constructing your skit is to answer the two basic questions pertaining to purpose: "What's the point?" and "Where's the joke?"

Step 3: Frame of Reference and Point of View

This step is a key component in establishing the slant of your sketch or your "take" on a sketch idea. To return to our house analogy: if you're drawing blueprints for a house, this is where the specifications part comes in. It describes the mechanical needs, such as the number of beams necessary to support the structure and hold the framing together. In sketch building, point of view and frame of reference work in conjunction with the two preceding steps — category (what prompted you to write the sketch in the first place) and purpose (the point and joke of the sketch) — to help support and hold together your comedy piece.

How do you recognize point of view? In teaching sketch classes, I ask my students to fill in the blank in response to the following question: "It's my point of view because _____"

◆ That's my reality of it
◆ That's my opinion
◆ That's how it appears to me
◆ That's my attitude.

In other words, point of view represents your opinion or attitude toward your sketch idea.

Frame of reference, on the other hand, is based on your knowledge or experience of the subject or situation, and relies mainly on recall — the "been there/done that" aspect of selecting your sketch's slant. To clarify your approach, answer this question: "It's my frame of reference because _____"

◆ It actually happened to me
◆ That was my perceived experience of it
◆ I imagine it to be this way
◆ It's part of my belief system

In the "Too Much Shoulder Pad" piece, for example, my attitude or opinion about shoulder pads was: the bigger the pads, the better a woman looked. This became the point of view of the sketch. Based on my own experience, my frame of reference was my sudden compulsion to wear shoulder pads in all my clothing. Because of my dependence on this "flattering" new look, I subsequently developed an uncontrollable addiction to wearing the pads.

By identifying both my point of view and frame of reference with regard to shoulder pads, I added an essential component to the blueprint of my piece. I was then ready to move to the next step in sketch building: laying the foundation.

Step 4: Concept or Premise

The concept or premise of a piece provides the basic foundation — the metaphorical cement slab, if you will — for sketch construction. Without this foundation, everything you erect might come crashing to the ground. However, with the concept or premise of your sketch clearly in mind, you can address the fundamental question: "By what means will I reach my satirical goal?"

Before going on, let me first make a clear distinction between an idea and a concept or premise, so you don't confuse the two. In sketch writing terms, an idea is merely the starting point for a concept or premise; it's just a piece of something larger. A concept or premise, on the other hand, embodies or encapsulates the entirety of a sketch — the beginning, the middle, and the end. It's the piece of something followed through to delivery of the comedic goods.

The concept or premise, then, supplies an overview of the sketch, including consideration of the beginning, middle, and end; the situation at hand; and the circumstances surrounding it. At its creative best, your concept or premise provides an original, clever, intriguing focus for your piece, while also incorporating prior choices as to category (Step 1), purpose (Step 2), and point of view/frame of reference (Step 3).

How do you arrive at a concept or premise? First, add a

situation and a set of circumstances to the selections previously made in Steps 1-3 of the sketch-building process. To establish these two new elements, you'll need to define the who and/or what, why, where, and when of your piece. Second, after defining the 5 "W's", you'll need to identify an interesting spin, a different angle, a clever hook, or a surprising slant to build that information around. Obviously, this last part is the biggest assignment, and also the most difficult to do.

To say something in an original way, you'll have to get creative. I always encourage my students to explore different approaches and go beyond the obvious. In improv, we have a saying: "Heighten and explore; then discover something new." Let's return for a moment to the "Too Much Shoulder Pad" sketch for an illustration of this process.

As you'll recall, I had previously selected a category (my obsession); a purpose (everybody's wearing shoulder pads, and they're addictive); and a point of view/frame of reference (I'm wearing them in everything, and I need more). Now I needed to develop a situation and a set of circumstances for the above. To do that, I first answered the five "W's":

Who: Two fashionable women

What: Their addiction to shoulder pads

Where: A women's trend-addiction support group meeting

Why: They'd become so addicted, they couldn't control their urges and needed help

When: During their "Hi, my name is..." part of the meeting

The answers helped me to formulate a concept or premise consisting of a given situation and a set of circumstances. From there, I decided on my unique hook or angle: during the meeting, the two women would confess that in order to build up their shoulders and support their ever-escalating habit, they'd stuffed their clothing with a multitude of items. So at the completion of Step 4, I had established a given situation, a set of circumstances, and a unique hook. With this overview, I also had a rough idea of the beginning, middle, and end of my sketch.

One final thought about concept and premise: you might be interested to know that many full-length sketches have their origins in the fleeting moments of an improv setup. In other words, an audience (for a show or workshop) yells out the particulars — who, what, where, and the conflict — and bingo, that's the concept for a scene. The direction the scene takes from there depends on the opening dialogue and/or action of the improv players; and with anywhere from two to five actors in a scene, there's no real control over the ultimate outcome. (Like I said, though, the concepts generated in this format are often developed into full-blown sketches at a later point in time.)

As a sketch comedy writer, you'll be the one in charge of where you take your ideas, including development of concepts or premises. Even so, you can learn a valuable lesson from improv players: as you go about developing concepts and premises, be spontaneous. Let it flow. React and respond from one thought to the next. Be as free as possible. If you do this, you'll stimulate boundless creative energy — and a plethora of possibilities! And always keep in mind, concepts or premises are like the foundation of a house: they're the base upon which your sketch is constructed.

Reviewing Steps 1-4

Before leaving the first half of the "Fast and Funny Formula," let's go over what we've covered so far. In Step 1 of the sketch-building process, we discussed *category*, something that triggers a writer's desire to create a particular sketch. In Step 2, we focused on *purpose*, specifically the reason for the satire and what's funny about it. In Step 3, we defined *point of view* (attitude, opinion, etc.) and *frame of reference* (the "been there/ done that" aspect). And in Step 4, we looked at *concept* or *premise*, which provides an overview of the piece, including its beginning, middle, and end.

With Steps 1-4, we've completed the design or blueprint phase of the sketch building process, and now we're ready to move on to the actual construction of a comedy piece — Steps 5-8 of the formula.

Building the Project
(Actual Construction)

A Preview

By staying on track with the fundamentals thus far, you now have a strong base (category, purpose, frame of reference/point of view, and concept/premise) on which to build out your sketch. Just like in building a house, the actual construction of a comedy piece requires precision and attention to detail, because the components are very much interrelated and interdependent. Let me explain this in terms of the formula.

Steps 5 and 6 are concerned with the "how" of moving a comedy piece along from beginning to end — both the *general* aspects of sketch movement (Step 5) and the *specific* aspects (Step 6). After the general and specific components of the "how" are in place, the piece is then "filled" in with the exact words and actions to be used by the characters (Step 7). The final element of the sketch is the topper, the ending (Step 8).

Returning to the homebuilding analogy for a moment, the outside structure of the sketch (Step 5) is the frame of the house; the inside structure (Step 6) is the interior walls; the dialogue and action (Step 7) are the furnishings and wall treatments; and the ending (Step 8) is that final touch that signifies completion of the project. And like with a house, these elements must be precision crafted if the sketch is going to stand up to critical appraisal. So be sure to construct with care!

Step 5: The Outside Structure

Like all aspects of construction, erecting the outside structure of a sketch can be tricky. Once again, it's like framing a house: everything has to fit together properly as you go along. In addition, the structure must be strong enough to survive a certain amount of wear and tear.

There are four principles to keep in mind when you're creating your outside structure. If you follow them in order, each one will nail a part of your piece to the next in a logical way; and the end result will be to tighten and make specific the outline furnished by your concept or premise. As in previous exercises, you'll need to fill in the blanks as you move methodically forward.

Principle #1 is the principle of "There is/was...". And surprise! You've already done most of the work for this one. In the concept or premise exercise, you established the "who, what, why, when, and where" aspects of the sketch. Now that you've situated your audience, the principle of "There is/was" simply requires you to flesh out your concept with one additional element — the "how." Let me return to the "Too Much Shoulder Pad" piece for a moment.

We've got two fashionable women with an addiction to shoulder pads. They're at a women's trend-addiction support group meeting, because they've decided to seek help for their uncontrollable urges. It's the "Hi, my name is..." phase of the meeting.

As the sketch writer, I needed to figure out how to introduce my concept to the audience, given the above particulars of the situation. Applying Principle #1, I filled in the blank in the following way: "There are/were two fashionable women standing up together to make a joint confession as to their shoulder pad addiction during the 'Hi, my name is...' segment of a trend-addiction meeting."

When you're utilizing Principle #1, you'll want to think in terms of what the audience will first glimpse as the stage lights come up. Your audience should readily grasp what's about to transpire. By adding the "how" to the five previous elements, you've created a strong visual image for the audience; they have a picture of an "actual" situation. It's like the initial image on a movie screen, or the melody line of a song. In home building terms, it's the first few boards of the framing process, the ones you'll be attaching everything else to.

Now we're ready to apply Principle #2, the principle of "What if..." This principle allows us to bring something new to the sketch, to develop it further by adding ideas that are congruent with the concept/premise and the "how." In the "Too Much Shoulder Pad" sketch, I asked myself, "**What if** the two women confessed they'd begun using objects other than actual shoulder pads to achieve the ultimate shoulder lift?"

Principle #3, the principle of "And then...", stimulates further development of the sketch by providing additional creative options. This is how I filled in the blank for Principle #3: "**And then**, during their joint confession, the two women gradually reveal the extent of their addiction as they begin padding the shoulders of their jackets with an increasingly bizarre array of objects, which further underscore for the audience the out-of-control aspect of their addiction."

Through the application of Principles #2 and #3, we've expanded the creative possibilities for "filler" elements like dialogue, action, and the use of props, which we'll get to later in the sketch-building process. In the meantime, we've further developed and embellished our piece. Now we need to bring the sketch to a close.

Principle #4, the principle of "And so...", is designed to provide an ending for our comedy piece. Here's how I applied it in the shoulder pad sketch. "**And so** the two women go completely over the edge, stuffing themselves until they look like humongous linebackers; after which they confess they aren't cured yet, because they think they look great that way!"

The interesting thing about the four principles is you can use them more than once in the creation of a sketch, and they can be mixed and matched. For example, you could form the outside structure of your sketch by combining the principles in the following way: "There is/was..." (#1) and "what if..." (#2) and "what if..." (#2) "and then..." (#3) and "what if..." (#2) "and so..." (#4) "and then..." (#3)..and "what if..." (#2) "and then..." (#3) "and so..." (#4) "and so..." (#4) "and so..." (#4).

The point is, if you apply these four principles — using them once, mixing or matching them, anything that works, really — you'll be able to clearly and substantively frame your sketch. As I mentioned at the beginning of this section, everything must fit together properly as you move along. If you've carefully framed your sketch, it'll be less likely to fall apart at a later time, like in front of an audience! An additional bonus to using this format is you may well end up developing a sketch completely by accident.

According to the students in my sketch writing class, Step 5 is the most valuable of the eight steps. When you've completed it, you'll have a sturdy frame to attach the remainder of your piece to. In fact, from here on out, your work relative to crafting a sketch is fairly easy: it's simply a matter of filling in.

Let's move on, then, to Step 6 of the sketch-building process, creating the inside structure.

Step 6: The Inside Structure

In Steps 1-4, you carefully laid out your ideas, so you have a good idea of what's going to take place in your sketch. With Step 5, you began work on the "how" of getting from one point to the next using the four principles. Now it's time to get more specific about the "how" of your sketch: how to make things happen. To explain this step, I'll be borrowing a term from improv comedy called "beats" or "beat points."

Quite simply, beats or beat points are the pivotal points within a scene that move it along through events, situations, and actions to arrive at a logical, workable ending. As a general rule, **something new should be added or revealed with each beat point**; and the sketch should progress in "build" and/or intensity as it moves from one beat point to the next.

Beat points, then, tie one piece of the scene to the next, like the dots in one of those dot-to-dot drawings. They're the important transitions, ranging from subtle to obvious, that support your original concept and divide up the outside structure you created in Step 5. Like the interior walls of a house that separate one room from the next, beats define discrete spaces within the overall structure of a sketch, and also keep the various parts connected to the whole in some pattern that makes sense.

Keep in mind, though, that beats are different from the specific words and actions of the characters in your sketch. Beat points establish **what** will transpire during a sketch; they indicate, at the macro level, what the characters will be saying and doing at major transition points. However, the precise dialogue and micro-actions of the characters won't be added until Step 7. (For example, in Beat 2 presented below, you'll notice that the two women will be introducing themselves to the support group; however, you don't know yet what their exact words will be.)

Let's return to the "Too Much Shoulder Pad" piece for an illustration of how beats propel a sketch from point to point.

Beat 1:   The scene begins with the stage in darkness; we hear a voice describing the situation we're about to encounter.

Beat 2:   The lights come up. The women introduce themselves to the other support group members.

Beat 3:   Both women take turns saying something about their addiction, as they demonstrate for the group how terrific they look with padded shoulders.

Beat 4:   Still taking turns, the women illustrate how their addiction has worsened over time.

Beats 5-8: The commentary continues to shift back and forth between the two. With each beat, however, the ante is raised with the stuffing process and the momentum of the piece grows. Since we haven't yet added dialogue or action to the sketch, we don't know specifically what the characters will be saying or doing. What we do know, though, is there will be four more exchanges between the women (beats 5-8), and each episode will reveal something increasingly horrific about the direction their addiction has taken.

So, the beats or beat points that comprise the inside structure of a sketch, and the four principles ("there is/was...what if...and then...and so...") that form its outside structure are integral to the "how" of a comedy piece; they work in combination to propel it along. Recalling the house analogy: the outside structure is like framing; the inside structure is like walls that separate one space from the next, but also connect them to the whole.

Let's move on to Step 7, where you'll learn how to flesh out the beats of your piece with what I term "filler."

Step 7: Filler (Dialogue and Action)

This next-to-last step of the sketch-building process is often one of the most exciting, because it brings the piece to near completion. Here, you'll be adding two important "filler" elements: dialogue and action. Decisions about the precise words and micro-actions of the characters in the piece should evolve naturally from the choices you've made in the previous six steps of the sketch-building process. In fact, many students tell me that when they finally arrive at this point, the dialogue and action seem to practically write themselves. By contrast, many novice writers struggle unnecessarily, because they tend to want to do the "filler" first, without any advance preparation.

Before going on, let me remind you of the importance of beats (the inside structure). By carefully laying out the beats in advance of the dialogue and action, you've provided the logical connections that link one part of the sketch to the next.

With the transition points in place, you know in advance *how* your sketch is going to evolve and unfold. What you don't know yet is whether it'll be funny. **The element most vital to the humor of your piece is the specific words and actions of the characters.** Ideally, you'd like each line and action to garner a laugh. This isn't always the case, of course — you might have one, two, three, and then a punch — but I'd recommend writing every line with the idea in mind that it'll provide additional humor.

Let's go back to the "Too Much Shoulder Pad" sketch for a moment. When it was time to add dialogue and action to the piece, I tried to select humorous comments and activities that would build to a frantic pitch. Here's what I came up with.

Initially, the two women make small confessions. They talk about how they started with real shoulder pads, wearing them in all their clothing. As the sketch progresses, the women take turns revealing how their addiction has escalated over time. They admit they've begun using objects other than actual pads to give greater height and width to their shoulders; and the objects they confess to using are increasingly absurd.

The impact of the dialogue is heightened by the action that accompanies it: as the women speak, they show the support group (and the audience) the objects they've utilized; and then demonstrate the effect by stuffing the objects into the shoulders of their blazers. As the addiction steadily worsens, the objects become larger and more bizarre (for example, one woman steals the visor from her husband's sports car, cuts it in half, and puts half in each shoulder), and the shoulder heights rise accordingly. By the end of the piece, their shoulders are so stuffed with objects, the women look like hard core line-backers.

Now, suppose I'd constructed the scene so the women talked about their growing addiction, but didn't actually demonstrate the increasingly bizarre behavior they'd engaged in. If I'd done that, the piece might have failed to build in humor; the joke was strengthened by the action that accompanied the dialogue. When dialogue and action work in tandem in a sketch, the audience receives both auditory and visual cues, giving them more to laugh at.

There's no hard and fast rule for writing filler. For example, you might want to write all the dialogue first, and then select actions that would logically accompany those words; or reverse the process — action first, then dialogue; or, of course, write them simultaneously. Within the piece, you can mix and match: dialogue, then action; action, action, then a piece of dialogue. Your only real constraint is the appropriateness of your choices: they must evolve naturally from the characters and circumstances you've created in prior steps of the sketch-writing process.

Remember, you have a lot to fall back on. The starting point of the piece is a category (Step 1), which your characters can continually comment on. The answers to the two questions, "Where's the joke?" and "What's the point?" (Step 2), are important to keep in mind; so, too, are frame of reference and point of view (Step 3), which very often dictate where you'll go with the filler. And you have an overall concept (Step 4), plus an outside and inside structure (Steps 5 and 6), to further guide you in formulating dialogue and action.

So while I'm not claiming that dialogue and action are easy to come by every single time, I am suggesting that by completing Steps 1-6, you'll have primed yourself for Step 7. Remember, though, if you haven't built a solid structure for the sketch first, you won't have anything to "decorate" with dialogue and action.

Here are some helpful tricks and guidelines for the filler step of the process:

1. Keep the dialogue simple, quick, punchy, relative, and spontaneous.

2. Make sure the actions support the dialogue by being appropriate, clever, surprising and/or well-timed.

3. Use the fewest words necessary. Sketches should be short and quick. The longer they are, the bigger the payoff required at the end.

4. Don't overwrite. One too many actions or bits of dialogue and you'll stifle the piece, causing it to appear sluggish. And when you overwrite, the audience spends time culling out what's significant to the joke — time they could have spent laughing had the piece been better written. Remember: every word and action should have a reason for being expressed, as well as serving to enhance the point and the joke.

5. Use profanity only if it's appropriate to the piece. Personally, I prefer the Jerry Seinfeld philosophy of writing without profanity, and there are two good reasons for this: 1) it assures your comedy can be presented just about anywhere for anyone; and 2) it showcases you as a much cleverer writer. Some comics feel they must shock their audiences to make them laugh, but much of the laughter they generate is simply a nervous response by the audience. If you do decide to use profanity, make sure it's essential to the piece.

6. The dialogue and action should be representative of, and true to, the characters you've created.

7. Metaphorically speaking, step inside your comedy piece (house) and live in it for a while until it feels like a comfortable place to be.

8. Expect to write several drafts of your sketch. Rarely does a comedy writer turn out a final piece the first time around. You'll want to "work the piece" until the timing, flow, and punch appear optimal. After a while, you'll begin to know when your work should be opened to the public, so to speak.

9. Filler in comedy is like the balance found in a good lyric, piece of prose, dramatic soliloquy, or one-liner. Again, in time, you'll know what works.

10. One last note: the measuring stick I use for my own work is whether I consistently laugh each time I hear the dialogue and see the action. When I do, I've passed my personal test. If the piece pleases me only intermittently, something isn't firing; and I know I need to do more work on it.

Now, I'm not suggesting every sketch must be riotously

funny. In fact, I've seen audiences respond well to comedy pieces that weren't exactly belly benders. However, I do think in order to please and satisfy an audience, a sketch must be well-written, carefully crafted, and possess both substance and build.

Returning to our homebuilding analogy, if your comedy piece has a solid foundation and structural integrity, the dialogue and action serve as the decor. Like the wall hangings, paint colors, carpets, and furniture in a house, the dialogue and action in a sketch reflect the individual, personal touches of the "decorator" (you!). With their inclusion, the piece is nearly finished and ready to be put on display.

Now we're ready for the final step, the ending.

Step 8: The Ending

In Step 7, with all the preparation you've done up to that point, some of you might find the dialogue and action almost write themselves. The task in Step 8, though, is quite a bit trickier; the fact you've followed the formula and solidly built your piece doesn't guarantee that this last part — the ending — will always work. And if your ending doesn't work, it tends to negate everything that precedes it.

You'll want to keep in mind the ending has to substantiate the rest of the piece. It has to make the final statement. It has to have the satirical bite. The punch. It has to satisfy the audience. It has to provide justification for the piece and bring resolution to it. And it has to tie together all the elements that came before it, particularly the dialogue and action. In fact, sketches are really just condensed stories; and like with any story, the ending has to provide closure.

Sketch comedy is similar to other types of comedy — stand-up, sitcoms — when it comes to the importance of endings. The last thing said in any sequence is the payoff; it's what the audience has been waiting for. So the ending of a comedy piece does double duty: it must complete the story and garner the biggest laugh or elicit the strongest emotional response.

How do you write an ending that delivers the necessary

kick? Finding a way to surprise the audience is the surest way. A strong ending catches the audience off guard; they don't see it coming, so they're unprepared for it. You can use the "and so..." principle from Step 6 to guide you here. Consider the message of the piece and ask yourself what would need to happen ("and so...") to justify making this statement in the first place. Be creative with your answer to that question.

Another way to devise a workable ending is to reverse the process: decide first on the finish for the sketch, and then back up into the ending with text that would logically support it. In terms of the formula, you'd be doing Step 8 first, then working methodically through Steps 1-7, keeping your ending clearly in mind throughout. I often craft my own sketches this way.

Remember: it's not unusual to search for some time before arriving at a suitable ending. I always advise my students to write an initial ending, followed by three or four alternates. Then they can put the piece up, try the different endings, and see which one delivers the biggest bang.

That's precisely what I did in the "Too Much Shoulder Pad" sketch. I spent a lot of time and made a variety of attempts to find an idea that would complement and cap off my joke. Eventually, I went with my "gut level" feeling about what would work. Here's how I decided to end the piece.

As you'll recall, two women were taking turns confessing with great shame, how their addiction had escalated over time, while simultaneously demonstrating to their support group the increasingly bizarre objects they'd used to expand their shoulder size. I decided the strongest choice for an ending — one that would continue to service the joke and deliver the biggest kick — would be to show how far these women were from being freed of their addiction. So the last lines of the sketch went something like: "...We know we're not cured yet...just this morning I stuffed myself silly, looked in the mirror, and said, 'God, I look great!'". The audience went crazy!

The "Too Much Shoulder Pad" piece was later named one of the best "Comedy Sketches of the Year" by the *Los Angeles Times*, and I'm convinced the strong ending had a lot to do with that award. As a matter of fact, I always tell my students to measure the success of a sketch not by the number of laughs it receives up to the ending, but by how the audience reacts the instant the piece is over. If the applause is weak, the ending is weak. Audiences are a great indicator of whether or not your stuff works. Let's look at some examples.

Suppose the audience laughs heartily throughout your sketch at all the strategic beat points, but the laughter dies out at the end of the piece. In that case, you can bet the audience felt deprived and disappointed by the ending. On the other hand, your piece might chug along slowly with a laugh here and a laugh there, and then be salvaged by a really good ending. Audiences are far more forgiving of a weak piece with a strong ending — a payoff that makes the wait worthwhile — than they are with the reverse. If you find yourself in a strong piece/weak ending situation, you're clearly in trouble and will need to keep rewriting until you get the desired response.

As a general rule, then, endings require a great deal of thought and manipulation. I know many writer/directors who verify endings by testing their pieces on stage in front of a preview audience. With my own sketches, I always note the final reaction of the audience, because it's the truest barometer of the strength or weakness of the ending.

To create a strong ending for your sketch, you'll want to keep the following points in mind:

1. Put your greatest creative emphasis on how you end your sketch.

2. Experiment with several endings until you arrive at the strongest and the best.

3. Gauge the success of your ending by how the audience responds to it. Try to base that assessment on an audience composed of people who are strangers to you; friends and family are apt to be biased.

4. When you read your ending, or view it on stage, ask yourself whether it consistently amuses you.

5. Make sure the ending substantiates your overall purpose for doing the piece in the first place.

If you've completed every step of the "Fast and Funny Formula" and devoted considerable energy and effort to the final step, in particular, you should be ready to present your sketch. One word of caution, though: you may need to make changes as you put your piece on stage and run it. Many sketches — even after the final draft — require additional reworking and revisions. Be open to that idea. And if you're planning to submit your sketch to agents or specific shows, first make certain you're deeply satisfied with the final result.

Now You're Ready

So you've followed the "Fast and Funny Formula" and learned a lot about how to build a solid comedy piece. You've gone from the blueprint phase (category, purpose, point of view/frame of reference, concept/premise) to actual sketch construction, including moving a piece along using the four principles and the beat points, filling in with dialogue and action, and adding the final punch, the ending. (Incidentally, you'll get even more practice with these terms in Chapter 11, when we break down sample sketches into the eight components of the formula, using the worksheet found in Chapter 13.) Since the formula itself is based on improv comedy, let's augment your sketch-building "tool-kit" with some additional guidelines borrowed from improv theories and technique, as presented in Chapter 9.

Before moving on, though, there's one final task in this section. Now that we've thoroughly deconstructed the "Too Much Shoulder Pad" piece, it's time to reassemble the eight major elements that make up the final product — the completed sketch. As you'll see, the old adage "The whole is greater than the sum of its parts" definitely applies here!

Please turn to the following page for the beginning of the sketch.

Kerr/Too Much Shoulder Pad/8-5-90

VOICE-OVER
(MALE VOICE, IN A CONFIDENTIAL WHISPER)

With new and addictive tendencies on the rise in this country, upscale communities have become a hotbed of controversy. Let's listen in on a support group for one of the nation's trendiest addictions...

LOUISE

Hi, my name is Louise ...and I too, suffer from...too much shoulder pad. It all started for me when I got my first blazer at Nordstrom's **(PUTS ON BLAZER)** and it had these nice little soft, supple shoulder pads in it, and my husband said "Gee, you look thinner! Have you lost weight?" I knew I needed more!

RUBY

My name is Ruby...for me, it all started at my image consultant's office. She put a dress on me...I thought it looked great. She said "It needs some shoulder pads, dear." I said, "I don't do that kind of thing, I'm not that kind of girl." She said, "Oh, go ahead, just try one pair." So I buckled under the pressure and put them in **(PUTS IN ONE PAIR)**... and I was hooked!

LOUISE

At first, it was just gonna be on weekends, and then I started using everyday, **(PUTS IN A PAIR OF SHOULDER PADS BENEATH THE BLAZER)** I mean first, it was just my blouses and then all of a sudden it became my aerobics wear, **(PUTS IN ANOTHER PAIR OF SHOULDER PADS)** and not just my dresses and my jackets and things, it became everything, my shawls, my vests, and pretty soon my full length aprons...and...I even put them in my nightgowns!

RUBY

A few weeks later, I found out I was pregnant, and as I went out here, I had to go up here! So I started adding at first **(ADDS ONE MORE PAIR OF SHOULDER PADS AND PUTS ON JACKET WITH PADS ALREADY IN)**. Just a couple of inches on either side, eventually up to five inches, and finally I was up to about five pounds on each side. I turned around one day and knocked my neck out...had to wear a brace. My husband said, "What happened?" I said it was a car accident... because you lie when you have...too much shoulder pad.

LOUISE

I tried to stop, but I couldn't. One day, one of my kids yelled to me from the bathroom "Hey Mom, Mom! Can you bring me some toilet paper, I'm out!" I said, "Okay." So I went to the cupboard and picked up a couple of extra rolls and I looked at them...and I couldn't resist **(SHOVES IN A ROLL ON EACH SIDE)**, I just shoved them in...I didn't care...because you don't care when you have too much shoulder pad!

RUBY

I was becoming obsessed, so I went to see a psychiatrist. But all I could think of as I sat in the chair was how great his throw pillow would look on my left side and how wonderful his back rest would look on my right! Then I had the baby and things got worse. I started with Pampers Small, went to Medium, Large, and finally, **(TAKES DIAPERS OUT OF BAG)** Pampers Extra Large...forty pounds and over! I put them in **(DOES SO)**...it wasn't enough!

LOUISE

I was in a business meeting and in walked the Vice-President...and hers were bigger than mine...so

I ran to the bathroom, borrowing every dime I could on the way and I grabbed those things **(PULLS OUT TWO SANITARY PADS, RIPS OFF STRIPS AND SHOVES INTO JACKET WHILE TALKING)** and ripped off those things...those self-adhesive strips...they're fabulous...they'll stick to anything!

RUBY

I was cleaning my kid's room one day...came across her favorite stuffed animal, **(LIFTING ONE TWEETY AND THEN THE OTHER OUT OF BAG)** Tweety and Tweety! They were thick, they were round, oh, I put 'em in **(DOES SO, LAUGH-ING LIKE A MANIAC)** it STILL wasn't enough!

LOUISE

I was driving down the street with my husband and the sun was just blaring through the windshield...all of a sudden he reached up to put his visor down...it was gone...there was nothing there...and he said, "What happened to the visor?"... **(TAKES OUT TWO HALVES OF A VISOR)** and I said "I don't know, I haven't seen it!" **(NOW ALSO LAUGH-ING LIKE A MANIAC AS SHE SHOVES THE VISOR PIECES INTO HER BLAZER)** I stole it!... because you steal when you have too much shoulder pad!......but you know, that wasn't the worst of it...the worst of it was the last time I was at the grocery store. I mean, for a long time I had everything under control, you know...a kiwi here, a banana there...and then all of a sudden one day I was walking out through the produce depart-ment... **(BECOMING INCREASINGLY FRAN-TIC)** and I see that guy stacking those melons...and I don't know what happened...I hit the door and all of a sudden I snapped, I turned that cart around, ran back, grabbed that guy by the green apron and said "Look, **(AS SHE SHOVES TWO MELON HALVES INTO HER BLAZER)** just give me the honeydew and nobody gets hurt!!"

RUBY

For me, the bottom fell out one day in the pediatrician's office...there was a little boy sitting there, about four years old...he had a cold...snot running all over his face...I didn't care...he had on these plush little slippers...I ripped them off his feet **(PULLS OUT BERT & ERNIE SLIPPERS)** ...Bert...and Ernie! They didn't match...I didn't care... because...**(WITH UNLEASHED FURY AS SHE SHOVES SLIPPERS IN)** when you have too much shoulder pad...YOU DON'T GIVE A SHIIIIIIIIT!

(GRIPPING EACH OTHERS' HANDS, NEARLY SOBBING)

That's why we're here. We know we have a problem...and we know we're not cured yet, because, I don't know about you, Louise, but just this morning, **(CALMER NOW)** I got up, got dressed, stuffed myself silly...went to the mirror, looked and said...

BOTH

(POSED IDENTICALLY WITH HANDS ON HIPS AND WITH A GASP) God, I look great!!!

LIGHTS

Using the Theories and Techniques of Improv Comedy to Bolster the Formula

The audience for an improv comedy performance sees a group of actors on stage taking suggestions from the audience, interpreting those ideas, and creating sketches on the spot. To its viewers, improv comedy appears freewheeling and totally spontaneous. However, as the actors themselves are well aware, improv comedy is deeply rooted in theory. There are guidelines — very specific guidelines — the actors must follow if the sketches they're creating on stage are going to hold together and entertain the audience. If even one of the actors violates these rules, the integrity of the piece can break down, resulting in a sketch that's dull, unfunny, and unworkable — an improv actor's nightmare.

The guidelines of improv comedy serve the actors, of course, but can be useful to non-actors as well. Think of it this way: as you're building your sketch by following the eight-step formula, you're essentially operating just like an improv player — you're making it up as you go along. The only significant difference is you can go back and edit your work, while the improv actor must live with what he or she created the first time around.

From the many improv terms and guidelines available, I've chosen 14 that are particularly relevant to sketch building.

The first two will help you with construction of the overall sketch.

1. **Beginning/Middle/End.** Just like with sketches, improv scenes must always have a beginning, middle, and end. The beginning situates the audience; the middle addresses an issue or conflict; and the ending resolves it and brings closure. With a lifespan of only 1½ to 3 minutes per scene, improv actors are constantly thinking in the beginning/middle/end format.

   As you're laying out your sketch, you'll want to note whether you have the above elements in place. I've seen some scenes that open strongly but don't seem to travel anywhere; others that fail to clearly introduce a conflict or issue, so it's difficult to understand what the authors were trying to express; and still others that just fade out for lack of a definitive ending.

2. **Creating Into Certainty.** With its brief lifespan, the improv scene must be introduced quickly and definitively, in specifics rather than generalities, rapidly situating the audience. My improv students quickly learn this rule: the first line out of an actor's mouth or an initial action should lay the entire foundation for the scene. You can easily adapt this rule to sketch comedy as well.

The next several terms will assist you with elements of dialogue and action in your comedy piece.

3. **Give and Take.** Action and dialogue go back and forth among the actors to keep the scene in balance and the actors at parity. In improv, no one actor is a star; the players work as a team.

4. **Division of Responsibility.** Each actor takes a percentage of the work in a piece, so the burden never falls on one individual, nor does any actor dominate the scene. Dividing up the work in this way tends to bring harmony and balance to the sketch.

By keeping #3 and #4 in mind, you'll be more likely to give each of your characters a vital role in the sketch.

5. **The "Yes, and…" Theory.** Improv actors always "go

with" what is introduced or set forth by the other player. When everyone is progressing down the same trail, things always thread together.

An example? Let's say there's a sketch about two guys going bowling. One says, "Let's go bowling." The other says, "No." Right away the scene has to be restructured to take it somewhere else. Granted, the second guy could say, "Let's go fishing instead." If the first guy then says, "No," the scene is just spinning in a circle. On the other hand, if the two characters are in a "Yes, and..." mode, the piece can develop safely as each character "goes with" the other's comments.

6. **Adding Information.** This term is related to the "go with" concept, and means exactly what it says. As the scene progresses, each character simply adds something sequential to the last thing said or done, or to the last idea held by another character. If a piece is constructed in this fashion, it should move along and unfold in a tight, orderly fashion. In addition, this is a great device for keeping your sketch continually on track.

7. **Refusal and Denial.** In improv terminology, if one actor ignores another, he **refuses** her; if an actor undercuts or changes direction on another, she **denies** him. If your characters are in a state of Refusal or Denial, it may be difficult to move your piece along. The idea is to always have the characters "go with" what is happening, from line to line and action to action.

   In the "Too Much Shoulder Pad" sketch, one woman could have minimized the other's addiction — a denial; or began talking about an addiction other than shoulder pads — a refusal. In either case, the scene would break down, and it'd be difficult to know where to go from there.

As you're writing a sketch, consider the outcome if your characters were in agreement and "went with" each other as the scene transpired. Certainly, the scene would flow more easily. Of course, the characters can disagree, too, but you'll still want to avoid having them refuse (ignore) or deny (change direction or undercut) one another. In other words, they could argue, but still follow up on — "go with" — each other's comments.

Gary Austin, one of my my mentors and a well-known director, says that agreement ("yes, and...") and conflict (man vs. man, man vs. himself, man vs. nature) always run along parallel tracks in improv. The following exchange provides an illustration of this principle:

Bob: We've been married for 10 years.

Martha: Yes, it has been a decade, hasn't it?

Bob: I want a divorce.

Martha: Not as much as I do.

Bob: I'm taking the piano.

Martha: Fine. Then I'll take your beloved golf clubs.

Bob: Wait a minute.

Martha: All right, but not a second longer.

As you can see, both players are in agreement in the sense that they're adding information or "going with" one another's statements; and yet, they're very obviously in a state of conflict as well. This is an important guideline to remember when developing your sketches.

8. **Re-Using Information.** If your characters reiterate something introduced previously, this will serve to thread together one or more themes in the scene or sketch.

9. **Assumptions and Revelations.** When characters in an improv scene bring up something from the past about or between one another, those comments are called assumptions. And revelations, as you might guess, occur when characters reveal their innermost thoughts and feelings. Both devices can be used to drive forward the characterizations with dialogue that adds depth to the sketch.

An understanding of the next three improv terms will assist you in fleshing out scenes.

10. **Critical Moment.** A critical moment in improv occurs when you take the usual to the unusual, and is often

used to provide a big punch ending in the form of a surprise, such as when the scene suddenly takes a strange or bizarre turn. Actors relish opportunities to introduce a Critical Moment, because it's a great way to end the scene with a bang. That's not to say you can't have a critical moment at any point in a scene; but it's commonly found at the very end.

11. **Pattern Making.** This is another interesting component used in fleshing out scenes. A pattern can be anything that requires either occasional or constant attention on the part of the actors. For example, it might be hot in the room, but the window won't stay open, so different actors are constantly lifting up a window that keeps falling down; or perhaps the actors are standing around a barbecue, trying to talk shop, as they continually fend off clouds of smoke from the grill. Most repetitive actions that interrupt actors repeatedly during a scene are classified in this category. I tell my students to think of a boiling pot on the stove; they have to keep going back to it.

12. **Actional Choice.** This term refers to changing the course of a scene through action rather than dialogue. The techniques can serve to surprise the audience and add some flavor to the scene, thus providing the writer (or actor) with an additional device for moving the scene along.

The final two improv terms apply to you, the sketch writer.

13. **Trust.** In improv, our number one rule concerns trust. We have to learn to trust both the process and one another. So in terms of your writing, you'll need to learn to trust yourself enough to let go and dive into your writing, and also to trust that the pieces will help write themselves.

14. **Commitment.** In improv, no matter how weird the components of the setup we're given by the audience, we make it work; we solve the problem. Maintaining a deep sense of commitment will help give you impetus in the face of inertia. Remember: you've given careful thought and planning to your piece; so even when it doesn't feel like it's working, stay committed. Make your characters

commit to the process through you.

I hope you'll find these "tools" from the world of improv as valuable as I have. With every sketch I've written, I've borrowed basic guidelines or scene components from improv comedy to assist me in creating and fleshing out my material. The neat thing about improv is it allows you to run wild, making it up as you go — but within the framework of guidelines, boundaries, and an overall structure that help ensure the scenes will work.

A final word of advice here: take some of your original ideas — in the purpose and category stages — and improvise them out. At any point in the sketch-building process, if you find yourself feeling stuck or stagnant, use some of the improv fundamentals to get you out of your mental ditch. Experiment. Go beyond the obvious. Believe it or not, the quickest way to reach the finish line is often by playing — spontaneously, freely, creatively. Enjoy the process!

Writing Sketch Comedy for a Specific Character

As mentioned previously, the categories listed in Step 1 of the formula — topical, human nature, obsessions, and so on — are good launching points for your comedy sketches. An alternative approach to the writing process is to start from the point of a particular character (or characters) and then build out from there, tailoring the piece to the nature or personality of your "star." There are several ways to develop sketches based on specific characters.

One method is to write for an already established character. For example, with Paul Reubens' "Pee-wee Herman," the character's eccentricities — his neuroses, beliefs, attitudes, and conflicts — provided the starting point for the story lines of the television series and several movies. And in the case of Julia Sweeney's "It's Pat," many sketches written for the character begged the question of whether Pat was male or female.

On the other hand, you may want to create and develop original characters. One approach is to write characters specifically for the types of pieces featured on a particular show, such as *"Saturday Night Live"*, *"In Living Color"*, or *"Mad TV"*.

A second approach to creating and developing original characters is to write for someone whose acting range you're familiar with. In other words, since you already know the scope of characters he or she can play, you can develop new characters based on the actor's specific abilities. For the past 18 years

I've worked with an actor, LizAnne, and together we've developed at least a dozen really strong characters for her. These characters include Betsy Braille, a blind pastry chef with a TV cooking show (imagine the possibilities!), and Lulu Hutchinson, a has-been stage actress who unexpectedly encounters an audience and invites them to call out scenes from previous performances, which she then attempts to re-enact. In both cases, the set dialogue and most of the improvised beats were written explicitly for the characters, based on the considerable talents and range of the actress portraying them.

A third approach to creating characters for sketch comedy is to develop original characters and then pass the sketches along to your favorite actor, or submit them to a show or comedy troupe. And finally, if you have acting ability and are comfortable performing, you may want to write for yourself. Everyone has subpersonalities they can turn to for inspiration in creating new characters. You can explore a part of yourself, bring it forward, and have it express.

Another reliable source of ideas for characters, whether writing for yourself or someone else, is people watching. I think all of us are characters in our own right. If you spend enough time in crowds of people — say at Disneyland, the zoo, baseball games, etc. — you're bound to observe some interesting personalities in action. You can then develop characters based on your observations of people's physicality, voices, attitudes, likes and dislikes, fears, and nuances of behavior. Or you can play "Mr. Potato Head" by mixing and matching people's characteristics, combining them to form unusual, intriguing characters.

Before creating a character, though, be sure to get clear on whether you're trying to develop a realistic person or a caricature, or exaggeration, of one. Examples of caricatures would include "Pee-wee Herman," "Pat," and Steve Martin and Dan Ackroyd's "Wild and Crazy Guys" from "*Saturday Night Live.*" Real characters, on the other hand, are either impersonations of actual people — for example, Gilda Radner's Barbara Walters, Eddie Murphy's Stevie Wonder, or Phil Hartman's

Ed McMahon — or replications of people whom we could conceivably encounter every day on the street, but whose personal characteristics make them good satirical targets. Examples include Julia Sweeney's "Mea Culpa," a guilt-ridden assistant to a Catholic bishop, or the "Anal Retentive Chef" of Phil Hartman.

When writing for a particular character — caricature or real — be sure to identify the beliefs, values, innermost thoughts and feelings, background, dreams and goals, life experiences, and essence of the "person" you've created. The more substantial and fully developed the character, the more interesting the sketch you'll be able to construct from it.

Sketches written for particular characters come in a variety of configurations. These include: single character sketches; sketches with one dominant character and several supporting or subordinate characters; and sketches showcasing two to five distinctive and equally strong characters.

Single character comedy pieces are often used in sketch shows to fill the time it takes for other actors to get dressed for upcoming scenes. When employed in this way, they're called "cover changes" or "up and ones." There are a number of situations that lend themselves to cover changes. For example, the Orange County Crazies did a takeoff on Mr. Rogers (and his beautiful neighborhood) in which he was describing to his young listeners how to make bombs from common household items. Since the real Mr. Rogers often presents his shows in this format, the conversion to a single character satire was an easy one.

Cover changes can also be derived from situations such as a character hawking a product, appealing to a school board, making a political speech, etc. In addition, there are pieces in which a character moves about the stage, interacting with objects and furnishings and commenting on them; and even solo pieces with action but no dialogue, like England's Mr. Bean. (For an example of a cover change, see the sketch entitled "Child Support" in Chapter 11.)

At the opposite extreme, I've seen sketches with three to

five characters, all of whom were so strong that the skit became the launching pad for a full-length play written around those characters. As you can see, there are many ways to build out your sketches from the starting point of a particular character or characters.

It's certainly possible to write a sketch that focuses on a particular situation (the "what") rather than the characters involved (the "who"). Some writers simply create the situation, and then leave the interpretation and delivery of the lines to the discretion of the actors. Many beginning writers, in fact, routinely get stuck on the "what" of a scene, and need to be guided to the "who" and the "why." However, writing for specific imaginary people tends to anchor a comedy piece in the "who" of sketch construction, thus taking it to a very human level.

In general, by including characters in your sketches, you breathe life into your sketch, provide a nucleus for the sketch itself, and protect it from being predictable and ordinary. As a matter of fact, some writers find this type of writing so inspiring, they end up specializing in writing "to" particular characters. And sharply drawn characters can be real crowd pleasers, too. If you're lucky enough to create a character like Cassandra Peterson's "Elvira, Mistress of the Night," you can literally live off the proceeds generated by that single effort for the rest of your life!

One last piece of advice: really strive to make your characters original. When you consider that no two people in the world are exactly alike, that all of us have many "little people" residing inside of us, and that you can combine characteristics from several different sources to form a single character, the choices and possibilities for creating original characters are seemingly endless.

You can find this out for yourself by trying some of the assignments I give my writing students. For example, I require them to write one skit around an original character; another for a famous person, living or not (see the "Edgar and Emily" sketch in Chapter 11); and still another focusing on the interrelations of family members, each having distinctive traits, as they struggle to cope with a specific crisis. This latter exercise, in particular, will give you practice in creating various characters, while at the same time paying attention to the design and construction process outlined in the "Fast and Funny Formula."

PART THREE

Working The Formula

Sketches That Do Work
and Why

Now that you've learned the "Fast and Funny Formula" and followed the "Too Much Shoulder Pad" piece through each of the eight steps of the sketch-building process, let's test the formula by applying it to some additional examples. The following sketches have been performed in shows that were well received by critics and audiences alike. The sketches will be presented in their entirety, and then we'll be breaking them down, step by step, to see how closely they follow the eight-step formula.

The first sketch was written soon after the Oklahoma City bombing, and has a duration on stage of less than one minute. The title is "The Terrorist."

(Special note: The header line, which gives the author's name, sketch title, date, and draft number should appear in bold-faced type at the top of each and every page of the finished script; but to conserve space in the sample sketches, I'll be listing it just one time per sketch. You can look at the "Too Much Shoulder Pad" sketch at the end of Chapter 8 for the correct format. See page 56.)

Kerr/The Terrorist/4-22-95/First Draft

<u>[INTERIOR OF INTERROGATION ROOM. THREE FBI AGENTS SURROUND A PRISONER BEING HELD FOR SOME APPARENT TERRORIST ATTACK. INTENSITY IN THE AGENTS. PRISONER IS CALM AND UNCONCERNED WITH THEIR "THREATS."]</u>

AGENT #1

You know, I'm getting real sick and tired of you...terrorists!

AGENT #2

You know, frankly, buddy, one of these days you're gonna tell us everything we want to know!

AGENT #3

We're gonna take away your privileges. No water!

AGENT #1

No privacy!

AGENT #3

No women!

AGENT #2

Maybe the death penalty, huh?

AGENT #1

How about...no media coverage?

<u>[THE PRISONER SUDDENLY SITS UP, CONCERNED. THE TENSION AND ANGUISH BUILD UP IN HIM AT THE MERE THOUGHT]</u>

AGENT #2

How about... no *"Hard Copy?"*

AGENT #3

<u>[TAUNTINGLY]</u> No *"20/20."*

AGENT #1

No *"Inside Edition."*

AGENT #2

No *"Current Affair."* [THEY'RE SCREAMING IN
HIS FACE NOW.]

AGENT #3

"Dateline!"

AGENT #1

"60 Minutes!"

AGENT #3

"Nightline!"

AGENT #1

"Extra!"

AGENT #2

"American Journal!"

PRISONER

[COMPLETELY COLLAPSING INTO TEARS,
GRABBING AN AGENT IN EACH HAND
AND PULLING THEM INTO HIM FOR
MERCY] No! No !Please! I beg of you! Anything,
[WHINING LOUDLY NOW] but not thaaaaat!

[LIGHTS]

Follow along with me now as I break down the sketch into
the eight components of the formula. Remember: the more
comfortable you are with the formula, the more prepared you'll
be to begin writing your own pieces. Let's get started.

Step 1 – Category. Something topical, and something that
bugged me and pushed my emotional buttons. (I was
infuriated at how much press coverage the perpetrators
of this crime were getting, and how much they seemed
to thrive on the publicity.)

Step 2 – Purpose. My satirical point was that terrorists get great press coverage. The joke was in imagining how a terrorist would react if the coverage were taken away.

Step 3 – Point of view. My opinion was the terrorists were getting off on being the center of attention. My frame of reference was my perception after watching TV news coverage of the events.

Step 4 – Concept. Three government agents threatening a terrorist with removal of his privileges.

Step 5 – Outside structure. There was... a terrorist and three government agents... what if... these agents threatened to take everything away from him... and then...they got so frustrated they started threatening to take away various national television shows that would provide him with press coverage... and so he began to lose his composure at the thought of losing the limelight.

Step 6 – Inside structure. Beat 1: Scene opens with Agent #1 expressing disgust. Beat 2: Agent #3 suggests taking away privileges. Beat 3: Agent #1 suggests taking away media coverage. Beat 4: Prisoner becomes concerned. Beat 5: Agents take turns naming news programs — in effect, upping the ante.

Step 7 – Filler. The dialogue includes lines like "We're gonna take away your privileges. No water!" and further threats such as "No '*Hard Copy*'" and "No '*20/20*'" as the agents up the ante in terms of eliminating privileges. Actions of the characters include the intensity expressed by the agents, the growing concern displayed by the terrorist, and the terrorist grabbing the clothing of the agents.

Step 8 – Ending. The terrorist turns into a complete wimp at the thought of losing his media coverage and pleads, "Anything...but *not thaaaaat!*".

The next example is also a fairly brief sketch, which takes place in a therapist's office. The title is "Psychiatrist Visit."

Kerr/Psychiatrist Visit/6-12-95/First Draft

[INTERIOR OF DOCTOR'S OFFICE. DOCTOR HAS NOTEPAD AND PEN IN HAND AS HE TALKS ON THE PHONE, OCCASIONALLY GLANCING QUIZZICALLY AT HIS PATIENT, A 12-YEAR OLD BOY]

DOCTOR

Tell Brad's mom I'll call her back after this appointment...okay... thanks. Todd?

TODD

What?

DOCTOR

Were things any better this week?

TODD

Not really.

DOCTOR

What happened?

TODD

Nothing any different from any other week.   Oh, except one of my friends, Scott Kennedy...

DOCTOR

Yes.

TODD

Well, we all had to get up and talk about some of the things we'd do to make the holidays more meaningful with our families this year — see, it's a special project and everything — and Scott started talking about his mom and dad again and—

DOCTOR

And...?

TODD

And the things they do. Well, it's always so interesting to everyone, even Miss Davis. And like all the other kids are sitting there nodding like they know, 'cause they do the same things with their moms and dads... ya know, they all relate... except me... I hate how it is with my parents... I hate my life... it's so embarrassing. It sucks. Why can't I be like all the other kids? Why can't my family be just like all of theirs?

DOCTOR

Todd, we've been through all of this before. I know it's hard. It's not easy for children, especially in these times and for someone your age. I know how it must be when you feel so different from the other kids who, in one way or another, tend to constantly remind you of your situation.

TODD

I'm such an outcast. I always feel so uncomfortable when everyone starts talking about family things...

DOCTOR

Look: life is full of challenges. And oftentimes we can't make life go the way we want it to. Try to think of it in a positive way: you'll be so much better off as an adult for having had to make adjustments — for accepting things the way they are. You can't control your parents, Todd. You can't make them conform to the way other kids' parents are.

TODD

[LOSING CONTROL, STARTING TO GET VERY UPSET, AND BEGINNING TO CRY] I hate my parents! Do you know what it's like to handle vacations and Christmas and my birthday? My mom, my dad, my mom, my dad. [GESTURES TO ONE SIDE, THEN THE NEXT] I don't even want my friends to come over for dinner or spend the night or anything. God, the stress of it all, day after day...

DOCTOR

I understand...

TODD

That's why I have to come here every week. The stress of it all...

DOCTOR

So what else do you think you can do?

TODD

Nothing. Just keep hoping that some day they'll get sick of each other, or end up hating each other, and they'll get a divorce, too. **[PAUSE, AN AFTERTHOUGHT AND SMILE AS HE EXITS]** I'm thinking positive!

[LIGHTS]

The breakdown for this sketch goes as follows:

Step 1 – Category. Something that pushes my buttons, is topical, and intrigues me.

Step 2 – Purpose. The satirical point is that social trends have made children with divorced parents more common than those from intact families. The joke comes from looking at the situation from an adolescent's viewpoint: his intact family is different, so it's a source of embarrassment to him.

Step 3 – Frame of reference. My own childhood and those of my three children. I've learned that adolescents want desperately to be just like their friends. My point of view is that's my opinion about what's going on today for many adolescents with married parents.

Step 4 – Concept. A 12-year old boy goes for his weekly therapy appointment to discuss the difficulties he encounters due to his parents' marital status.

Step 5 – Outside structure. There's... a 12-year old, all-American boy who's disturbed and distraught over his parents' relationship... and what if... he confides to his psychiatrist that it's terribly difficult for him to handle his parents' situation... and then... we learn that his parents' situation is somehow different from that of his friends' parents... and then he begins to describe what it's like... and so... we find out his despair stems from the fact that his parents are married, while all his friends' parents are divorced.

Step 6 – Inside structure. Beat 1: Doctor asks Todd about his week. Beat 2: Todd describes how he doesn't fit in at school because his family isn't like other kids' families. Beat 3: Doctor tries to reassure him. Beat 4: Todd's unhappiness escalates as he discusses the embarrassment and stress he's feeling. Beat 5: Doctor prods him to come up with an alternative form of behavior. Beat 6: Todd gives his version of a "positive" approach to the problem.

Step 7 – Filler. Dialogue fills in the doctor/patient exchanges between an adolescent boy complaining about his problems with his parents' marital status, and the doctor trying to reassure him that everything will turn out okay. Examples include: "I'm such an outcast. I always feel so uncomfortable when everyone starts talking about family things..." and "You can't control your parents, Todd. You can't make them conform to the way other kids' parents are." The action is minimal, but includes the doctor initially talking on the phone while scrutinizing his patient, and the patient becoming increasingly emotional as the session goes on.

Step 8 – The Ending. The surprise twist comes when we find out the source of the patient's anxiety and embarrassment. We think he's been talking about how hard it is to come from a broken home. Instead, that's what he's longing for, so he can be like all his friends whose parents are divorced.

Now that we've looked at two relatively brief sketches, let's move on to three longer pieces. After reading each sketch through to the end, use copies of the worksheet provided in Chapter 13 to break down the sketch according to the "Fast and Funny Formula." Then you can check your answers against the explanations I've provided at the end of each sketch. Since there's always more than one way to look at things, don't be too surprised if your answers vary slightly from mine. The main goal here is to get practice in using the formula.

Kerr/Nip 'N' Tuck/1-12-92/First Draft

[LIGHTS. AT A FAST FOOD-TYPE WINDOW WE SEE A CLERK DRESSED IN SURGICAL SCRUBS. HE HAS A HEAVY FOREIGN ACCENT. EACH CUSTOMER ENTERS IN A MAKESHIFT PROP CAR.]

CLERK

Welcome to Nip 'N' Tuck. Can I take your order, please?

FIRST WOMAN

Yeah. Am I right, is this a drive-through cosmetic surgery place?

CLERK

Yes, ma'am, that's correct.

FIRST WOMAN

Oh great. I'd like to order a lower body value pack, please. And does that include a tummy tuck?

CLERK

Yes, ma'am, that's included.

FIRST WOMAN

Oh great. How about throwing in a couple of calf implants?

CLERK

That will be $2000 extra, ma'am.

FIRST WOMAN

Okay. That will be fine.

CLERK

Would you like some anesthesia with that?

FIRST WOMAN

Of course!

CLERK

Local or general?

FIRST WOMAN

General.

CLERK

Okay, ma'am. That will be $6500 at the second window.

FIRST WOMAN

All right. Thanks.

CLERK

Thank you.

[SECOND WOMAN DRIVES UP TO THE WINDOW. SHE'S WAY OVERWEIGHT.]

Welcome to Nip 'N' Tuck. Can I take your order, please?

SECOND WOMAN

Yes. I have a coupon for a buy one/get one free liposuction, and I'd like to get my hips done.

CLERK

This coupon has expired, ma'am.

SECOND WOMAN

Umm. Well, just do my left one, then. It's bigger.

CLERK

Would you like some anesthesia with that?

SECOND WOMAN

Yes.

CLERK

Okay. How about our special this morning? It's a chin implant.

SECOND WOMAN

No. I have enough of those.

CLERK

Okay, ma'am. That will be $1500 at the second window.

SECOND WOMAN

Okay. Thank you.

[THIRD WOMAN DRIVES UP TO THE WINDOW. SHE HAS TWO KIDS IN THE BACK SEAT.]

CLERK

Welcome to Nip 'N' Tuck. Can I take your order, please?

THIRD WOMAN

Yeah. Can I have a Love Goddess combo, please? And can I have a dermabrasion instead of having my teeth bonded?

CLERK

Sorry, ma'am. No substitutions allowed.

THIRD WOMAN

Uh...how much is it on the side?

CLERK

That's $2000 on the side, ma'am.

THIRD WOMAN

Uh...not today. **[KIDS ARE BUGGING HER.]**
What's this week's Happy Plasty?

CLERK

Ninja turtle backs, ma'am.

THIRD WOMAN

Ohhhh, all right. We'll take a Donnatello and a
Michelangelo.

CLERK

Would you like an anesthetic with that?

THIRD WOMAN

No!

CLERK

Okay, ma'am. That'll be $7500 at the second win-
dow.

THIRD WOMAN

All right. **[TO HER KIDS]** Aw...shut up!

[YOUNG MAN DRIVES UP TO THE WINDOW.]

CLERK

Welcome to Nip 'N' Tuck. Can I take your order,
please?

YOUNG MAN

Yeah. I want to get the super sex change.

CLERK

Would you like a breast augmentation with that?

YOUNG MAN

Yeah. I guess so.

CLERK

Small, medium, or large?

YOUNG MAN

Uh...large.

CLERK

Okay. Would you like to try our special this morning? It's a chin implant.

YOUNG MAN

Yeah. I'll take a double.

CLERK

Would you like some anesthesia with that, sir?

YOUNG MAN

What kind do you have?

CLERK

Local or general.

YOUNG MAN

I'll take one of each.

CLERK

Okay, sir. That'll be $20,000 at the second window.

YOUNG MAN

Would you throw in a nose job?

CLERK

That'll be $2000 extra.

YOUNG MAN

Whatever.

CLERK

$22,000 at the second window.

YOUNG MAN

All right. Thank you.

[DOCTOR WALKS OUT TO MEET CLERK SITTING AT DRIVE-BY WINDOW. THE LAST PATIENTS HAVE DRIVEN OFF FOR SURGERY. DOCTOR IS ALSO DRESSED IN SCRUBS.]

DOCTOR

Well, Bob. How're we doing today?

CLERK

We're doing real good, Dr. John.

DOCTOR

Ah, great...

SECOND WOMAN

Hey! Hey! Hey!

[SHE ENTERS AND GETS THE DOCTOR'S ATTENTION.]

I was just in here for a liposuction on my left hip and you did my right hip and look, you gave me a ninja turtle back.

DOCTOR

You didn't order a ninja turtle back?

SECOND WOMAN

No! I did not!

[FIRST WOMAN ENTERS, BANDAGED AND ANGRY.]

FIRST WOMAN

I am very upset. I need to speak with the manager.

SECOND WOMAN

I came in for a lower body value pack and I got a... nose job. I like my nose. And my breasts have been reduced too. My husband is going to be furious.

[THIRD WOMAN ENTERS, VERY ANGRY.]

THIRD WOMAN

Hey! You're in a lot of trouble, mister. **[SHE SHOWS HIM HER KIDS. POINTS TO SON WHO NOW HAS BIG BOOBS.]** I can't send him to school like this! We didn't get what we ordered, and also you gave me a fat ass!

[YOUNG MAN ENTERS, IRRITATED.]

YOUNG MAN

Excuse me...excuse me. There seems to be some problem here.

DOCTOR

Yes?

YOUNG MAN

When I ordered a breast augmentation, I really thought there were going to be two. **[HE SHOWS HIS CHEST WITH ONE BOOB.]** And what did you guys do to my ears?

DOCTOR

You didn't order Spock ears?

YOUNG MAN

No.

DOCTOR

Okay. We can take care of all of this right now. Don't get worried. Just move on down the corridor **[HE MOTIONS THEM OUT]** to operating room E. And while you're waiting... free refills at the collagen bar.

FIRST WOMAN

I hope they can fix this.

THIRD WOMAN

I hope so, too, lady. You're going to need it. You look like hell.

[THEY ALL EXIT. DOCTOR RETURNS TO ORDER TAKER.]

DOCTOR

Bob! Bob! How many times have we gone over this, Bob?

CLERK

I know, Dr. John. I told them to go to the second window. She went to the first. I don't know. She's stupid.

DOCTOR

[LOOKING EXASPERATED] The first window, first. *Then* the second window. And *all* sex changes *always* go to the third window.

CLERK

Sorry, doc.

DOCTOR

Forget it. From now on *I'm* going to work the windows. Scrub up and *you* go operate on them.

CLERK

You want me to do O.R.?

DOCTOR

Yes. Go!

CLERK

Aw...I hate doing surgeries. Man!

[DOCTOR TAKES PLACE OF CLERK AT DRIVE-BY WINDOW. CAR PULLS UP.]

DOCTOR

[ADOPTING SAME HEAVY ACCENT AS
CLERK] Welcome to Nip 'N' Tuck. May I take
your order, please?

[LIGHTS]

Let's go through the eight steps of the formula again.

Step 1 – Category. Something absurd and something topical, too.

Step 2 – Purpose. The satirical point is that plastic surgery is becoming so commonplace, and the procedures so streamlined, that outpatient clinics may one day be as ubiquitous as fast food restaurants. The joke is in taking the analogy further, having the order taker mix up the plastic surgery requests just like a fast food worker mixes up the burger orders.

Step 3 – Point of view/frame of reference. My point of view is I imagine plastic surgery will become this widespread; and my frame of reference comes from the experience of going to fast food restaurants and occasionally receiving someone else's order instead of my own.

Step 4 – Concept. Four cosmetic surgery patients order and receive procedures at a drive-through plastic surgery center.

Step 5 – Outside structure. There's... this drive-through cosmetic surgery center... and what if... patients drive up to a window to place their surgery orders... and then... the clerk directs them to various windows for a specific procedure... and what if... the order taker isn't very bright and sends them to the wrong windows... and then...the patients return, very angry about the mixed up surgeries...and so... the doctor, frustrated with the clerk's ineptitude, decides to trade places with him.

Step 6 – Inside structure. Beat 1: The clerk waits at a drive-through type window to take plastic surgery orders. Beat 2: First woman drives up and places order. Beat 3: Second woman does the same. Beat 4: Woman with kids drives up and places order for herself and the kids. Beat 5: Young man pulls up and places order. Beat 6: Doctor comes out to chat with clerk. Beat 7: First woman comes in and angrily confronts clerk and doctor. Beats 8-10: Each patient reappears, angry about mixed-up surgeries. Beat 11: Doctor confronts clerk. Beat 12: Clerk blames problem on patient. Beat 13: Doctor orders clerk to do the surgeries and takes his place.

Step 7 – Filler. Most of the dialogue is a takeoff on the dialogue we encounter at fast food restaurants, such as "Welcome to Nip 'N' Tuck; may I take your order, please"; and customer requests for things like substitutions, combo platters, and Happy Plasties; and the doctor trying to placate the patients by sending them to the collagen bar for free refills.

Specific actions include the patients driving up to and away from the window in prop cars, the children of the Third Woman fighting in the back seat, the four patients angrily confronting the doctor and clerk and then walking toward operating room E, and the doctor taking his place at the drive-through window.

Step 8 – The Ending. After the doctor sends the clerk to the O.R. to perform surgery, he takes his place at the drive-through window and adopts the clerk's heavy accent as he greets the next customer in line.

A popular trend of the early nineties was movies-of-the-week or full-length feature films based on "real life" stories. The following sketch was written in response to that trend.

Kerr/Buy A Gun...Get An Oscar/2-14-93/ First Draft

[INTERIOR OF GUN SHOP. SAM STANDING NEAR THE COUNTER READING A COPY OF "ENTERTAINMENT WEEKLY." SALESMAN HAS BACK TO COUNTER, TAKING INVENTORY. MAN (ROBERT) ENTERS THE STORE, ANXIOUS, NERVOUS, AND DEPRESSED.]

                    SALESMAN
Can I help you?

                    ROBERT
Yeah... I guess so... I mean... Yeah... I want to buy
a gun.

                    SALESMAN
Oh, okay. What kind of gun?

                    ROBERT
[LOOKING AT DISPLAY CASE] Well... I'm not
really sure... I don't know... there's so many here...

                    SALESMAN
Well, here I got a nine millimeter Beretta
semi-automatic, or over here, I got a .44 Magnum...
hey, here's a .38 Special...or... maybe you'd like a
.357... hey! We got a great deal... Uzi automatic
assault weapon...

                    ROBERT
[CONFUSED] I don't know...there's so many...

                    SALESMAN
Well, tell me... is this for long range? Or close in?

                    ROBERT
[GESTURING, HOLDING HIS POINTED
FINGER TO HIS HEAD] Close in. I mean, I think
that's what I need.

[MAN (SAM) RAISES HIS EYES OVER THE MAGA-
ZINE WITH A LOOK OF INTEREST, SMILES, THEN
LOWERS HIS EYES BACK DOWN TO THE MAGA-
ZINE.]

                    SALESMAN
[HOLDING A GUN] Well, here's a nice little
piece. Real popular lately.

                    ♦ 93 ♦

> ROBERT

What is it?

> SALESMAN

It's what we call a Saturday Night Special. It's $49.95. Holds six rounds. Accurate up to 50 feet. Snub nose, easy to conceal. And, it holds its resale value, and the barrel will stand up to 5000 rounds before it needs to be rebored.

> ROBERT

Resale? Rebored? I'm only going to use it once.

> SALESMAN

Will this do it for you, then?

> ROBERT

Yeah, I guess so.

> SALESMAN

How many shells do you want?

> ROBERT

Hey, I said I'm only going to use it once.

> SALESMAN

Well, here's a box of 24. That'll be a total of $52.75.

> ROBERT

Thanks. **[PUTS GUN IN POCKET AND TURNS TO EXIT]**

> SALESMAN

Come again soon.

> ROBERT

No...I don't think so.

[SAM FOLLOWS ROBERT TO THE DOOR AND IN-TERCEPTS HIM.]

SAM

Excuse me...I couldn't help but overhear you over there, and... uhhh... you're not thinking about doing something to yourself with that gun or anything, are you?

ROBERT

Well, actually I am. I just got laid off. I was the best waiter Denny's ever had. Both my kids are in trouble at school. My wife left me...for another woman. My car was repossessed. I just spent the last $50 I had to buy this gun...

SAM

And you know, son...that might have been the best investment you ever made.

ROBERT

What? What are you talking about?

SAM

I got a little deal I'd like to make with you.

ROBERT

Deal? What do you mean, deal?

SAM

You don't want to use that gun on yourself.

ROBERT

I don't?

SAM

No. Let me just run four words by you: "ABC Sunday Night Movie."

ROBERT

Huh?

SAM

Look... have you ever thought about being in show business?

ROBERT

Show business? What...

SAM

You know... books... miniseries... movies... tours... big interviews... Oprah... Geraldo... ever think about winning an Oscar?

ROBERT

Gee, show business, an Oscar... I never thought...

SAM

[PULLS OUT CELL PHONE, DIALS A NUM-BER, SPEAKS INTO PHONE] Hey, Sid, it's me. Bring the team. I think I've got the property we've been looking for. **[PUTS THE PHONE AWAY]** Now, listen, kid... before you do anything rash, I want you to meet some friends of mine. I think we can do some business with this story of yours.

ROBERT

What... what story are you talking about?

[THE "TEAM" ENTERS; SAM PULLS OUT "PAPERS" FOR ROBERT TO SIGN]

FRANKIE

Oh, is this the property?

SAM

Yeah...I think he's our guy.

RUSS

Great...I just heard Paramount's looking for a new package: a three-picture deal with a book and a possible docudrama series.

FRANKIE

Great...but, who's he gonna shoot?

ERIC

How about Joey Buttafuoco?

RUSS

Nahhh...three networks have exhausted all the rights already for options for sequels.

FRANKIE

Oh, I know, how about Al Gore's girls, you know, blond, all-American...

RUSS

Nahhh... but politics is good, hasn't been done for a while... I think I can get six figures.

SAM

Six figures...

ERIC

No, the spin's too tough on that. Small town Tennessee doesn't sell.

FRANKIE

How about Quayle?

RUSS

Nahhh...there's no ratings in that anyway; we need a generic type...

ERIC

Oh, like the Texas cheerleader mom deal...

FRANKIE

Yeah, you know. Maybe a bank president or K-Mart clerk.

ERIC

No, the headlines are all love triangles, you know? We need a Jean Harris, Lana Turner...

RUSS

You know, a celebrity hasn't been done in a while.

FRANKIE

No. That's so Hinkley.

ERIC

So Mark David Chapman.

FRANKIE

We need a whole new side. Oh, I know. A former yuppie who goes berserk!

ERIC

Yeah, we could use you were abused, right? Fights back!

RUSS

Gentlemen! Gentlemen!

ERIC

I definitely see sitcom potential in this.

RUSS

Seven figures.

SAM

Seven figures...

[EVERYONE BEGINS YELLING AT ONCE, LOBBYING FOR ATTENTION, HIGHER VOICES, MORE INTENSE]

Oh, Sir! Sir! Sir! Sir!

ROBERT

[STEPPING AWAY FROM THE CROWD] You guys are all NUTS! I don't want to hurt anyone; I just don't want to suffer any more. I don't...

ERIC

Sure you do...do you have any idea how much money you can make from this? Why, you're just a regular guy from off the street, probably from an abusive family, broken home...

ROBERT

NO, NO, NO!!! **[ROBERT BACKS AWAY AS THE OTHERS PURSUE HIM. IN A PANIC, HE GRABS A GUN AND SHOOTS THEM ALL DEAD. SALESMAN APPROACHES HIM CAUTIOUSLY]**

SALESMAN

[CALMLY, DELIBERATELY ESCORTS ROBERT TO THE COUNTER] Now, son...just give me the gun... good... **[SALESMAN PICKS UP PHONE, DIALS, SPEAKS INTO PHONE]** Marty, it's me. Yeah. Hey, listen. I think I've finally got that deal...

[LIGHTS]

This is how that sketch breaks down:

Step 1 – Category. Something that makes a strong impression on me and is topical, too.

Step 2 – Purpose. The satirical point is if you buy a gun and shoot enough people, you become eligible for a career in show business. The rather bleak joke of the piece is that people are willing to exploit others in order to make those seven-figure movie deals.

Step 3 – Point of view. That's the situation as it appears to me. My frame of reference is the plethora of TV movies and feature films based on "real life" stories.

Step 4 – Concept. A down-and-out guy visits a gun shop one afternoon to find the right weapon to do himself in, but a Hollywood agent intervenes.

Step 5 – Outside structure. There's...this suicidal guy who goes to a gun store to buy a weapon so he can end his life...and what if...while he's shopping for one, he runs into a Hollywood agent...and then...the agent tries to talk the guy out of shooting himself...and then...the agent calls his buddies, who rush over and try to talk the suicidal guy into killing a larger number of people to make it a more film-worthy event...and then...the guy gets so confused and agitated, he kills all of them...and so the gun salesman seizes upon this "golden opportunity."

Step 6 – Inside structure. Beat 1: Man enters store and is approached by salesman. Beat 2: Salesman shows him a variety of guns, but continually misunderstands the man's reason for buying the gun. Beat 3: Man makes purchase, but is stopped on the way out by Hollywood agent lurking in the background. Beat 4: Agent dangles idea of a film career in front of the man. Beat 5: Agent calls business colleagues, who rush over, and attempt to persuade man to do something more "meaningful" with his purchase, offering various suggestions of what that something would be. Beat 6: Man freaks out and shoots all of them. Beat 7: Salesman approaches gunman to calm him down and gain possession of the gun.

Step 7 – Filler. The trickiest part of the dialogue occurs in the initial exchanges between the suicidal guy and the salesman, as the salesman manages to miss all clues as to the guy's plan for using the gun, while the Hollywood agent understands perfectly and is poised to milk the situation for all it's worth ("Let me just run four words by you: 'ABC Sunday Night Movie.'") Dialogue continues with the agent's team debating strategies for eliciting maximum dramatic effect and dollars ("No, the headlines are all love triangles, you know? We need a Jean Harris, Lana Turner..."), and ends with the gun salesman's phone call. Action includes the Hollywood agent noting the exchange between the salesman and the suicidal guy, the guy indicating that he intends to shoot the gun at very close range, the agent's phone call, the "team" members lobbying for the guy's attention, the guy shooting the agent and his team, the salesman calming the guy, and then picking up the phone and making a call.

Step 8 – The Ending. The salesman makes what we assume is a 911 call. Instead, we learn he's calling *his* Hollywood contact.

The final full-length sketch, "Edgar and Emily," is a good example of what I discussed in the previous chapter: sketches written for specific characters. In this case the characters are two historical figures, Edgar Allan Poe and Emily Dickinson.

Kerr/Edgar and Emily/4-12-95/First Draft

[INTERIOR OF HOME. MOROSE-LOOKING WOMAN SEATED AT COMPUTER (WORD PROCESSOR) LOOKING RATHER INTENSE BUT DOWN. SHE'S DRESSED ALL IN BLACK. SOMEONE KNOCKS ON THE DOOR.]

EMILY

Oh, come in.

EDGAR

[MACABRE-LOOKING, AS HE ENTERS WITH A LAPTOP COMPUTER. HE, TOO, IS DRESSED IN ALL BLACK] Are you alone?

EMILY

Aren't I always?

EDGAR

Yeah.

EMILY

What do you want to write tonight?

EDGAR

Oh, I got this great idea for this "Raven" thing.

EMILY

Raven?

EDGAR

Yeah, I thought of a really good line on the way over...

EMILY

Raven? Is that a black bird?

EDGAR

Yes. It looks like a crow, only shinier, and they don't have...uh...attitude like crows. Now, listen; let me try this on you **[PULLING UP A FILE ON THE LAPTOP AND READING FROM THE SCREEN]**: "Once upon a midnight dreary..."

EMILY

I don't know, Edgar. You knew I'd love the "dreary" thing, but "Once upon a — *anything*" is a little too flighty for me.

EDGAR

Is that one of your bad puns, Emily?

EMILY

Pun? Is that the latest trend in neoclassical literature? I've never written a pun before. Is it a sonnet, prose...?

EDGAR

Don't do that bimbo thing with me, Emily. I know you're deeper than that. Try this: "That one word, as if his soul in that one word he did outpour"?

EMILY

What "one word"? You're losing me, Edgar.

EDGAR

"Till the dirges of his hope that melancholy burden bore of never...nevermore."

EMILY

Sorry, I don't get it. And, quite frankly, it's still not morose enough for me.

EDGAR

[FURIOUSLY TYPING] "But the raven still beguiling all my fancy into smiling."

EMILY

What? Now a smiling bird? What is it, schizo-
phrenic? Where the hell are you going with this?

EDGAR

"Straight I wheeled a cushioned seat in front of bird,
and bust and door..."

EMILY

What? Some guy's sitting, talking to a bird?

EDGAR

"Blackbird singin' in the dead of night"? **[SHE
GIVES HIM A DISGUSTED LOOK]** Well, try
this, Emily: "And so faintly you came tapping, tapping at my chamber door that I scarce was sure I
heard you — here I opened wide the door."

EMILY

Uh,**[CONSIDERS IT]** nah!

EDGAR

How about if I add: "Darkness there, and nothing
more..."?

EMILY

Darkness... well, that I like.

EDGAR

Yeah, well, it rhymes with "door."

EMILY

Yes, but you need a hook. You know, something like
a chorus, a refrain...

EDGAR

Oh! I got it! "Quoth the raven, 'Nevermore'"! I
could say that after every verse: "Quoth the raven,
'Nevermore'..."Quoth the raven..."

EMILY

After every verse? How many are you going to write?

EDGAR

18... 20...I don't know.

EMILY

That won't work, Edgar. You always overwrite... like that pit/pendulum thing. You better think ahead, especially if you self publish. It could be costly.

EDGAR

[DISCOURAGED] Ohhhh...

EMILY

But hey, now it's my turn. Listen to what I got! Been working on this all day: "My life closed twice before its close... It yet remains to see... If immortality unveil... A third event to me."

EDGAR

Jesus! Are you on that death thing again?

EMILY

[EMILY GETS UP. STANDING BEHIND HIM, SHE SLAPS HIM ON THE BACK] Oh! So a blackbird is real upbeat? **[LOOKS AT HIS COMPUTER SCREEN, SHE READS OUT LOUD]** Oh, and: "Thinking about this ominous bird...by the grave and stern decorum... ghastly grim... soul with sorrow laden... " Come on, Edgar! Like this is a Dickens thing?

EDGAR

Hey, you're the angel of death.

EMILY

Hey, don't pick on me. I always write about death, and...

EDGAR

Did you ever consider therapy or church, or something...

EMILY

Church! I got a great church poem! I wrote it yesterday: "Going to the chapel...gonna get mar-ha-ha-ried..."

EDGAR

[HE LOOKS AT HER INCREDULOUSLY]
Nah!

EMILY

All right...here's another: "I'm ceded... I've stopped being theirs... the name they dropped upon my face... with water, in the country church... is finished using now... and they can put it with my dolls... my childhood, and the string of spools... I've finished threading too."

EDGAR

What? Your face on a doll? **[HE STANDS BEHIND HER, PULLING TAUT HER FACE]**
What are you talking about? And oh, that martyr thing, Emily...it's so passe...so wearing... you're killing me!

EMILY

Really? Well... fine. Let's just go back to yours.

EDGAR

[EXCITEDLY] Okay...you'll like this. How about: "And my soul from out that shadow that lies floating on the floor...Shall be lifted... nevermore"?

EMILY

[PULLING A NOOSE FROM UNDER HER BLACK BLOUSE AND LEANING SIDEWAYS AS THOUGH SHE'S HUNG HERSELF]

You're boring me with that "nevermore" thing!

EDGAR

I like the "nevermore" thing!

EMILY

Yeah, but now it's too much. No one's gonna buy that, Edgar!

EDGAR

Yeah... I guess you're right. **[HE PACKS UP HIS LAPTOP, LOOKING DISCOURAGED]** Forget it.

EMILY

Why don't you finish that "Tales Of The Grotesque And Arabesque" deal; it's much more commercial.

EDGAR

I don't know... I'm not so sure that will go over either. I'll see you tomorrow night.

EMILY

'kay. **[EDGAR GETS UP TO LEAVE. EMILY READS FROM HER COMPUTER SCREEN AS HE STOPS TO LISTEN]** "Had I, a humble maiden... Whose farthest of degree... Was that she might... Some distant heaven... Dwell timidly with thee."

EDGAR

[GIVES HER A DISGUSTED LOOK AS HE PREPARES TO EXIT] God!

EMILY

Yeah! That's what I'm talking about.

EDGAR

Geez, Emily... are you going through the... change, or what... you're getting worse all the time! And **[POINTING TO HER COMPUTER SCREEN]** sorry; that'll never sell. That's *junk!*

EMILY

[DEJECTED] You're right. It's not exactly something you'd ever see in print.

EDGAR

[STILL HOPEFUL WITH HIS POEM, RECITING AS HE EXITS] "And the raven, never flitting... still is sitting... still is sitting... And his eyes have all the seeming of a demon's... that is dreaming..."

EMILY

[SHAKING HER HEAD] Sorry, Edgar...it's not exactly *classic*.

EDGAR

[EXITING] See you tomorrow. [BEHIND HER BACK NOW HE STICKS OUT HIS TONGUE]

EMILY

Tomorrow...

[LIGHTS]

The breakdown for this sketch follows, but don't forget: your answers may be slightly different from mine, and that's okay.

Step 1 – Category. What seems absurd, as well as secret thoughts and feelings, since I had always wondered what it would be like if such literary greats were hard at work together, creating their masterpieces.

Step 2 – Purpose. The point of the sketch is the imagined meeting of the two historical figures. What's funny about the meeting is the juxtaposition of the past (their fiction) and the present (their equipment, song fragments, anxiety about whether something will sell); their lack of support for one another; and the miscalculations they make about what will or will not succeed with the public.

Step 3 – Frame of reference. Based on my knowledge of the writings of these two authors, this is what I imagine would transpire if they got together. My point of view is this is how it appears to me.

Step 4 – Concept. Two great American authors from the past get together regularly, with their Powerbooks, to write and preview their work for one another.

Step 5 – Outside structure. There are...two great authors of American literature...and what if...they got together every night and wrote...and then...at these sessions they would try out their new creations on one another...and then...each denigrated the other's work...and so...they experienced a great deal of anxiety about whether or not their work would go over with the public.

Step 6 – Inside structure. Beat 1: Emily is alone, as usual, writing. Beat 2: Edgar enters and opens his Powerbook. Beat 3 and beyond: As they write on their personal computers, they converse, sharing lines from their work, and bickering about the results of their efforts. Final beat: Edgar packs up and gets ready to leave.

Step 7 – Filler. There's very little action in this piece. Examples include Emily hitting Edgar on the back, Edgar pulling Emily's face taut, and both characters toiling away at their keyboards.

In the dialogue, which is the heart of the sketch, lines from the famous works of each author are interwoven with modern text, including song fragments, references to the high cost of self publishing, and worries about whether or not something will be a commercial success ("Yeah, but now it's too much. No one's gonna buy that, Edgar!"). At the same time, the dialogue attempts to stay true to the perceived personalities of these two historical figures; for example, there are several references to Edgar's preference for the bizarre and morbid and to Emily's fascination with death ("Hey, you're the angel of death.").

Step 8 – The Ending. Edgar sticks out his tongue in a competitive parting shot at his dear Emily.

The final sketch is a brief piece that provides you with an example of a one-person sketch written as a cover change.

(See Chapter 10 for a full discussion of cover changes and sketches written for particular characters.) I won't be providing a breakdown of it, so this is a good chance for you to practice one on your own, using the worksheet from Chapter 13.

Kerr/Child Support/5-13-95/First Draft

[STAGE IS EMPTY. WE SEE A LIVING ROOM TYPE SET. PHONE IS PROMINENTLY PLACED. WE HEAR IT RINGING. WOMAN RUNS INTO THE ROOM OUT OF BREATH, LEAVING DOOR OPEN AS SHE ENTERS IN A STATE OF DISARRAY. SHE CARRIES HER PURSE AND BAGS UNDER HER ARM.]

WOMAN

[INTO PHONE] Don...oh! Oh, Skip... it's you... Hi... I thought you'd never get back to me. [SLIPS OFF HER SHOES, STARTS TO UNDRESS] I know, I realize that, but I don't think you understand what it's like for me... I know... I know... but you must hear my side of it... I mean, you're not involved on a day to day basis... you have no idea how much [SHE'S GOT HER CORDLESS PHONE, AND SHE'S REACHING OUT OF THE DOORWAY TO BRING IN A BUNCH OF BAGS FROM VARIOUS STORES: ANN TAYLOR, NORDSTROM, NINE WEST, ETC. SHE STRUGGLES TO BRING THEM ALL IN... SHE'S STILL TALKING] It really... costs. Yes, I know... I know that... but Skip, I can't raise Todd on that. I need more money... For what? For all kinds of things. For his [WITH EACH ANNOUNCED ITEM, SHE TRIES ON ANOTHER NEW THING SHE JUST BOUGHT. SHE'S PULLING ITEMS OUT OF THE BAGS FURIOUSLY AND EXCITEDLY] soccer and school supplies...and [SHE'S LOOKING AND ADMIRING HER NEW STUFF IN THE MIRROR] haircuts, and Boy Scouts... uh, swim fins...

hamsters... hell, I don't know... braces. It's always something. Oh, fine! You try to live on that. What??!!?? How dare you! I do not... I don't eith... ha! **[LOOKING AT NEWLY MANICURED NAILS]** I haven't done that for... for myself... for... God knows when the last time was. **[SHE'S STILL TRYING THINGS ON]** Well, hey, divorce is expensive! Oh, come on, Skip, how about just this month — **[HE OBVIOUSLY SAYS OKAY. SHE LOOKS AT HER RECEIPTS AND SCRAMBLES TO ADD THEM IN HER HEAD QUICKLY]**. How much? Um, how about another $500? Come on, Skip. Be a good dad! **[HE EVIDENTLY ASSENTS. SHE HANGS UP THE PHONE, GRABS HER PURSE, AND AS SHE OPENS THE DOOR, SHE TURNS BACK TO LOOK AT THE PHONE]** Cheap son of a bitch! **[SHE SLAMS THE DOOR BEHIND HER]**

I hope by this point you're starting to feel really comfortable with the "Fast and Funny Formula." In the next chapter we'll be looking at three sketches that didn't work, trying to figure out — in terms of the formula — where the authors went wrong. So let's move on to the don'ts of sketch building.

Sketches That Don't Work and Why

At the outset, I'd like to offer my heartfelt thanks to the three students who gave permission for me to use first drafts of sketches they prepared for my sketch-writing class. The following examples appear here in exactly the same format as when they were first submitted to me as class assignments. You won't see the sketches in any finished or revised form, since at the time of publication of this book, the sketches hadn't yet been revised or reworked.

BOOBS ARE US
Not Quite Right or a Matter of Checks and Balances

<u>INTERIOR: LILLIAN IS ON A TABLE WITH A SHEET OVER HER. DR. ZION LEANING OVER HER.</u>

L

"Dr. Zion, is this going to hurt?"

Dr. Z

"No Lillian you won't feel a thing. I'm giving you a local. This way we will really be able to adjust the size." <u>(HE OPERATES ON HER A LITTLE.)</u> "OK, I think they are looking good now. Let's take a look." <u>(DR. Z HELPS HER UP AND HOLDS</u>

UP A MIRROR.)

L

(LILLIAN LOOKS INTO THE MIRROR WITH DISGUST) "Now *this one* needs to be bigger and fuller on this side. It still doesn't match." **(DR.Z HELPS HER BACK DOWN)**

Dr.Z

"Ok." **(HE SAYS KIND OF DEPRESSED AND SETS HER BACK DOWN)**

(DR.Z WORKS ON HER SOME MORE)

"Now this looks good. Lillian I know you're just going to love them." **(HE HELPS HER UP AS HE SAYS...)** "Lillian, how about this?"

L

"NO!,NO!,NO!!!! NOW THIS SIDE IS BIGGER! Oh my God! Add more! ADD MORE!!! Balance these damn things! **(SHE LOOKS DOWN AT THEM DISGUSTED AND SHAKES HER HEAD)** "FIX 'EM!!!" **(SHE QUICKLY SLAPS HERSELF BACK ONTO THE TABLE)**

Dr.Z

(SADLY TRIES TO HELP HER BACK AND GET ADJUSTED ON THE TABLE) (HE OPERATES ON HER AGAIN AND THEN SETS HER BACK UP) "How about now?"

L

"OK, it's looking better in size, but the nipples. **(SHE SHAKES HER HEAD)** They just don't stick out far enough. I can barely see them at all." I want some that definitely... **(SHE SHAKES HER HEAD, THINKING OF THE RIGHT WORD)** ... say hello."

Dr. Z

"OK. I see what you are saying. **(HE HELPS HER BACK DOWN)(DR.Z WORKS ON HER A LITTLE MORE)** "Now Lillian, THIS IS IT!" He says smiling. **(HE HELPS HER UP)** "Take a look."

L

(LOOKS, SMILES AND THEN FROWNS WITH A BIG LOWER LIP OVER HER UPPER LIP.)

Dr.Z

"Oh, Lillian, what's wrong now?"

L

"It's my face. It doesn't fit the size of my breasts."

Dr.Z

"What do you mean?"

L

"It's my ears. Look at them they need to be much larger. Please help me Dr.Zion."

Dr. Z

"OK Lillian, I can fix them. Don't you worry. Let me help you lay back down." **(SHE LAYS BACK AGAIN WITH HIS HELP) (DR.Z HELPS TO MAKE HER EARS LARGER)** "Well, what do you think now Lillian?" **(AND HE SETS HER UP)**

L

(SHE SITS UP AND LOOKS AT HER FACE. HER EARS ARE ENORMOUS.) "Something still isn't right...It's my nose...it's my nose. You have to balance it out with my ears. Please help me. I really want everything to be perfect. I want to walk into a room and have everyone in the room really notice me." **(SHE LAYS BACK DOWN AGAIN)**

Dr.Z

(WORKS ON HER ONCE AGAIN) "How's ev-
erything now Lillian?" (HE HOLDS THE MIR-
ROR TO HER FACE WHILE SHE IS LAYING
ON THE TABLE)

L

(SHE LOOKS HER FACE OVER) "Hummm.
You know I think you finally got the right balance...
the perfect look... You did it Dr. Zion! Thank you
so much!"

(LILLIAN GETS UP FROM THE TABLE, WITH HER
BACK TO THE AUDIENCE GRABS HER PURSE AND
TURNS AROUND TO LOOK AT HIM BEFORE SHE
GOES OUT THE DOOR. SHE LOOKS LIKE MR. PO-
TATO HEAD.)

"Good-by Dr.Zion. Thanks again."

(JUST AS SHE OPENS DOOR AND IS LEAVING. DR.
ZION'S SECRETARY COMES IN AND GLANCES AT
LILLIAN AS SHE IS WALKING OUT THE DOOR AND
THEN DOES A DOUBLE TAKE.)

Sec

(SAYS TO DR.Z AFTER LILLIAN HAS
WALKED THROUGH THE DOOR) "Hey, is
she a famous star or something?"

Now, let's look at this sketch in terms of the eight elements
of the "Fast and Funny Formula."

Step 1 – Category. This piece is introduced with only minor regard for category. Possibilities include something
the writer's obsessed with, something that intrigues her,
pushes her emotional buttons, or is absurd. I guess I'd
place the sketch in the last category — something that's
absurd. However, since it's unclear to me what prompted
the writer to undertake the sketch in the first place, we're
already off to a shaky start. Remember: an identifiable
category provides the foundation for the sketch.

Step 2 – Purpose. The reason for the satire and what's funny about it are similarly unclear. Is the writer trying to make a point about doctors and their poor work? Or is she saying that we're never satisfied with how we look? The message is vague, and the title is misleading — the piece heads off in a completely different direction from what's announced in the title.

Step 3 – Point of View. Classifying the point of view is also a struggle. Is this the writer's point of view because it's her reality of the situation? It surely doesn't have much to do with attitude or opinion; and since the consequences don't follow from the circumstances, the point of view can't be based on the way things appear to be.

The frame of reference, too, is difficult to pinpoint. Certainly it's doubtful that the sketch could come from the "it actually happened to me" frame of reference. Perhaps the situation is the way the author "imagined it to be," in which case her imagination doesn't seem to be tied closely enough to reality for the sketch to make sense.

Step 4 – Concept. The concept might be something like: woman goes to plastic surgeon to have boobs evened out and ends up with other changes. That is, in fact, a workable premise.

Step 5 – Outside Structure. Here's where we run into some real problems, because the sketch goes from a real-life situation to something that seems like an animation idea. Look at what happens when we attempt to apply the four principles that form the outside structure: There is...a woman who goes to a cosmetic surgeon to have her breasts evened out... and what if... she didn't like them after he did them — or is it what if... the size wasn't right, or what if... she decided to change everything else so she could look like a children's toy? The "what if" is obviously muddled.

Moving on to principle #3, "and then": and then... she asked the doctor to match the size of her breasts with her face. What exactly does that mean? What does the size of her breasts have to do with the size of her face? The physical correlation doesn't make sense to me, and so the picture isn't coming together in my mind. In an additional "and then" she asks for further physical changes, but are we laughing yet? Are we servicing the joke? What exactly is the joke? As you'll recall from Step 2, we aren't even sure what the joke of the piece is.

When the sketch reaches the "and so" portion, the patient is finally satisfied with how she looks. Based on what, though? At the beginning of the sketch, the patient was very concerned with proportion and making her breasts look believably wonderful; but at the end, she's supposedly ecstatic about receiving a Mr. Potato Head look. That's a huge, unsupported leap of faith to ask the audience to take; it strains our credulity. Even worse, we see the joke — such as it is — coming right at us, so it's both weak and unsurprising at the same time. Believe me, the audience will not be pleased.

Step 6 – Inside Structure. Examination of the beats reveals a limited progression in build or intensity over the course of the sketch. As a result, the transition points generate little interest. The sketch is basically just a series of requests to have various body parts altered, and there's not enough going on to produce the sequences necessary to move the sketch along from pivotal point to pivotal point. Consequently, as an audience member, I'm having a hard time staying entertained by it.

Step 7 – Filler. Since there's not much of anything going on in the sketch, the possibilities for dialogue and action are rather limited. Without interesting filler, the piece is unlikely to be humorous, or to possess a distinctive voice or an inventive edge.

Step 8 – The Ending. Here's that "and so" problem again: I simply can't buy into the fact that at the beginning of the scene the woman merely wanted her breasts evened out, but by the end of it she was delighted to leave the doctor's office looking like a cartoon character. Instead of providing a big punch, the ending leaves me puzzled and disappointed.

Perhaps if the character had left looking like a completely different — but real — person, the sketch might have worked for me; of if she'd come in with some absurd feature, or a partial Mr. Potato Head look that then evolved into a complete Mr. Potato Head makeover, maybe I'd have been satisfied. As you can see, though, it's difficult to write a clever ending if the material that precedes it can't support one.

In critiquing this writer's work, it seems to me that she stumbled early on in terms of purpose. We needed to know both the point of the satire and what was funny about it in order to understand the piece. As I've said before, each portion of the comedy structure builds on the section before it; so if there's not enough support from the bottom up, it's hard for the piece to stand and deliver.

Is the piece a total loss? Definitely, not. I think the writer had the potential to do something very inventive here. Perhaps the character could have started out beautiful and ended up happily ugly, based on the satirical point that we often want to look like someone else and seldom appreciate who we really are. If the writer wanted to go in the cartoon direction, perhaps she could have had her character arriving as Bambi or Goofy and then departing as Mr. Potato Head. For another possibility, the doctor could have remade the patient to look just like his receptionist, since many cosmetic surgeons create the same looks for all their patients rather than making the effort to customize their jobs.

So there are a number of choices the author could have made at the beginning of the process that would have given her a stronger foundation on which to build her comedy piece. I certainly applaud her efforts, though. As you can see, it's not as easy as it looks to get all the elements in place and properly nailed together.

Let's move on to our second example, a sketch entitled "The Dis Comforter." Once again, I present it here in the exact form in which I received it.

THE DIS COMFORTER

[LIGHTS OPEN TO ANNOUNCER AND BED QUILT]

ANNOUNCER

Are you DIS gusted with out of work relatives sucking the life blood out of your happy home? Unable to DIS lodge them from your guest bedroom. Well don't DISpear, you can make them DIS appear with the NEW DIS comforter bed quilt. It works by making your house guests as uncomfortable as possible so they'll hit the floor running faster than Barbara Mandrel after scarfing a bag of Sunsweet prunes. The DIScomforter is DIS guised to look like any other blanket but is equiped with an arsenal of "guest" deterrants such as the mock frozen foot fringe complete with toejam. The cracker crumb inserts that work together with the heavy lead panels so your victem will have more poc marks that Edward James Olmos And let's not forget the wedgie weapon which lodges underwear so tightly in their slackin' butt they'll be walkin' around like they were the poster child enema research.

So call today to get your DIS comforter. Remember our slogan "You can't be missin' til you dissin'". The DIS comforter brought to you by DYS co. the people who brought you The Pocket Pool Protector and The Pick Your Nose home rhinoplasty kit.

[COMMERCIAL IS OVER. ANNOUNCER TURNS AROUND TO REVEAL ENORMOUS WEDGIE ABOVE HIS PANTS]

You know I'm kinda tired, I haven't been sleeping very well.

This idea had potential, but as you'll note, it didn't really go anywhere, at least in the first draft that we have here. And while the sketch follows the first several steps of the "Fast and Funny Formula," it just doesn't work overall. Before breaking down the sketch, I want to remind you about an important aspect of script presentation: if you want your script to appear professional, make sure you eliminate all typos and misspellings before you submit it somewhere. Let's take a closer look at the sketch in question.

Step 1 – Category. The category of "what bugs you" (*i.e.*, out-of-work relatives camped out in your guest bedroom) is readily apparent.

Step 2 – Purpose. Here, too, the writer was quite clear. The point of the sketch was to play with the opposite of how a bed comforter is usually viewed; that is, the product being hawked in the sketch decreases comfort rather than adds to it. The joke lay in the double entendre of joining the modern term "dis" with the word "comforter," keeping in mind the normal function of a comforter. So the purpose of the piece — often one of the toughest parts to put in place — was solid, and the writer had a direction in which to head.

Step 3 – Point of View/Frame of Reference. The writer's point of view was "that's how it appears to be" (in other words, that's what a dis comforter would be like); and her frame of reference was "I imagine it to be this way." So the writer has set us up for the idea that the dis comforter will be geared to making houseguests as uncomfortable as possible.

Step 4 – Concept. This is where the sketch starts to fail, in terms of the formula. At this point the writer should have been addressing the who, what, why, where, and when aspects of the sketch in order to clearly depict a given situation and set of circumstances; however, in the actual sketch these details are rather vague, at best.

Step 5 – Outside Structure. This wasn't too bad. Using the four principles, the outside structure would look like this: There's... a blanket called the dis comforter... and what if... it made sleeping an unpleasant experience... and then... you supplied it to your unwanted houseguests, who encountered many difficulties during the night... and so these visitors soon decamped. So the piece appears, on the outside at least, to have been adequately laid out.

Step 6 — Inside Structure. In terms of the inside structure of the beats, however, the writer really missed out on many opportunities to move the sketch along from clever example to clever example of how the dis comforter worked against the well-being of the people who used it. Instead, the comparisons and descriptions she gave were weak, unfunny, and didn't flow or thread together well. Most importantly, there wasn't much build from one example to the next.

From an audience standpoint, I think what they'd want to see are graphic examples of how the blanket worked to the detriment of unwanted houseguests; they'd want to see the damaging effects of a night's sleep — or lack of sleep — that a blanket like this would produce. Without clever examples to mark the transitions along the way and build the intensity (say, if the damaging results had become ever more bizarre over the course of the sketch), the skit tended to spin in circles rather than to progress.

Step 7 – Filler. Just like with the previous sketch, when there's a lack of distinctive pivotal points, good dialogue and action are hard to come by.

Step 8 – The Ending. Although the ending provided a bit of a laugh, it didn't really have a strong enough kick to justify having sat through the piece. As you already know, the steps of the formula build and overlap; it's hard to get to a powerful ending when what's leading up to it doesn't have enough build.

Here's the third, and final, sketch of this chapter. It's entitled "Drive-Through Comedy."

Drive-Through Comedy

[DRIVERS AND DRIVE-THROUGH SPEAKER BOX]

BOX
WELCOME TO JOKE IN THE BOX. MAY I TAKE YOUR ORDER?

DRIVER 1

YEAH, I'D LIKE TWO ELEPHANTS, A RABBI
AND A BEAR IN THE WOODS.

BOX

TWO ELEPHANTS, A RABBI AND A BEAR IN
THE WOODS. WOULD YOU LIKE ANY MEXI-
CANS WITH THAT?

DRIVER 1

NO, THANKS.

BOX

THAT'LL BE 3 DOLLARS AND 24 CENTS.
PLEASE PICK UP YOUR ORDER AT THE NEXT
WINDOW.

DRIVER 1

THANKS

**[EXITS TO WINDOW, WHERE HE PAYS, HEARS THE
JOKES, LAUGHS AND DRIVES OFF].**

BOX

WELCOME TO JOKE IN THE BOX. MAY I
TAKE YOUR ORDER?

DRIVER 2

YEAH, I'D LIKE THREE CATHOLICS, TWO
DOGS AND ONE BUDDHIST.

BOX

THREE CATHOLICS, TWO DOGS AND ONE
BUDDHIST. WOULD YOU LIKE ANY
JEHOVAH'S WITNESSES WITH THAT?

DRIVER 2

NO, THANKS.

BOX

THAT'LL BE 4 DOLLARS AND 78 CENTS.
PLEASE PICK UP YOUR ORDER AT THE NEXT
WINDOW.

DRIVER 2

THANKS

[EXITS TO WINDOW, WHERE HE PAYS, HEARS THE
JOKES, LAUGHS AND DRIVES OFF].

BOX

WELCOME TO JOKE IN THE BOX. MAY I
TAKE YOUR ORDER?

DRIVER 3

YEAH, I'D LIKE TWO CHEESEBURGERS, A
LARGE ORDER OF FRIES AND A CHOCOLATE
SHAKE.

BOX

I'M SORRY SIR, WE DON'T HAVE THAT.

DRIVER 3

EXCUSE ME?

BOX

WE DON'T SELL FOOD HERE. THIS IS JOKE
IN THE BOX. IF YOU WANT FOOD, YOU'LL
HAVE TO GO TO JACK IN THE BOX.

DRIVER 3

OH. WELL, WHAT DO YOU SELL HERE, ANY-
WAY?

BOX

JUST JOKES.

DRIVER 3

JOKES? ALL RIGHT, THEN, TELL ME A JOKE.

BOX
YOU'LL HAVE TO PAY FOR IT.

DRIVER 3
HOW MUCH?

BOX
WHAT KIND OF JOKE?

DRIVER 3
UH...HOW ABOUT...A DYSLEXIC JOKE?

BOX
THAT'LL BE 9 DOLLARS AND 21 CENTS.

DRIVER 3
TOO MUCH.

BOX
ACTUALLY, IT'S 1 DOLLAR AND 29 CENTS.
SEE, IF YOU WERE DYSLEXIC, IT WOULD
BE...

DRIVER 3
9 DOLLARS AND 21 CENTS, YEAH, I GET IT.
CUTE.

BOX
THAT ONE'S ON THE HOUSE. THE NEXT
WILL COST YOU.

DRIVER 3
ANY SPECIALS TODAY?

BOX
AS A MATTER OF FACT, WE ARE OFFERING
3 HELEN KELLERS FOR THE PRICE OF ONE,
ALL THROUGH THE MONTH OF MAY.

DRIVER 3

SOUNDS GOOD TO ME. WHAT WOULD GO
GOOD WITH THAT?

BOX

WELL, THERE IS A SPECIAL COMBO DEAL
WE HAVE; WITH THE 3 HELEN KELLERS,
YOU CAN GET 2 POSTAL WORKERS, 3 LES-
BIANS, AND 4 IRAQUI SOLDIERS ALL FOR 4
DOLLARS AND 31 CENTS. WE CALL IT OUR
HAPPY MEAL.

DRIVER 3

SOUNDS GOOD. I'LL TAKE IT. CAN I GET
ONE OF THOSE LITTLE TOYS WITH IT?

BOX

YES, FOR 99 CENTS, LIMIT ONE.

DRIVER 3

SHOULD HAVE GUESSED. WHAT DO YOU
HAVE FOR DESSERT?

BOX

WHAT ELSE? **[PRODUCES CREAM PIE
WHICH IS HURLED IN DRIVER 3'S FACE.]**

LIGHTS

This was a good idea, but the writer had difficulty fleshing
it out. Here's how the sketch breaks down according to the
eight components of the "Fast and Funny Formula."

Step 1 – Category. This sketch falls into the "what seems
absurd" and "what's topical" categories, since everything
seems to be going the fast food route.

Step 2 – Purpose. The satirical point of the piece is how,
with the way the world is going, express service will soon
affect everything (even plastic surgery, as we saw in an
earlier sketch). What's funny about the piece is the
incongruency of pulling up to a fast food-type window

only to find that jokes are the only thing on the menu.

Step 3 – Point of View/Frame of Reference. Point of view is this is the author's opinion about what will happen in the future; and frame of reference is that he imagines it to be this way.

Step 4 – Concept. People pull up to a fast food-type window to order jokes. This was nicely captured.

Step 5 – Outside Structure. The "how" of the piece causes some problems for the writer. There were... these people who wanted humor... and what if... they could get it by driving through a fast food-type outlet. Up to this point the piece is working, but when we get to the "and then," it begins to falter. Something additional is needed to service the joke; otherwise, the sketch lacks build.

Step 6 – Inside Structure. The beat points have the same problem as the "and then" portion of the outside structure: they don't progress and escalate, or move from one interesting juncture to the next. It's same ol', same ol'.

Step 7 – Filler. Here's the biggest problem with the sketch. Although the dialogue shows potential, it's too weak. The joke orders aren't definitive enough, and they're not very funny. In addition, we never get the payoff; that is, we hear the customers laughing, but we never get to sample the jokes ourselves. And there are no actions accompanying the dialogue that would serve to enhance the joke of the piece. When the writer suddenly changes direction and opts for a mistaken food order, the sketch takes an even bigger dive, because the transition doesn't fit with the build in intensity that the writer was attempting to create.

Step 8 – The Ending. The pie in the face makes a great finish. There are many possible ways to arrive at that particular ending, but this sketch lacked sufficient momentum to reach such an elaborate payoff. I said earlier that a strong ending can sometimes make up for weak material; however, that is not the case here.

As you can see from the three sample sketches, there's definitely an art to successful sketch building; but now there's a science to it as well, and that's where the "Fast and Funny Formula" comes in. If you write your own comedy pieces using the worksheet in Chapter 13 to guide you through the eight steps of the formula, you'll greatly improve your chances for producing sketches that work — comedy hits rather than comedy misses.

Part Four of the book takes you beyond the formula into areas like writing alone vs. collaborating, writing for critics vs. writing for audiences, handling rejection, maintaining your sense of humor and source of inspiration, and methods for packaging and selling your sketch comedy. In those chapters, I offer insights gained from my many years of writing experience. In addition, I provide practical tips that will help you, the writers of the future, make a place for yourself in the competitive world of sketch comedy writing.

The Worksheet

The worksheet on the following two pages can be used to break down other people's sketches into the component parts of the "Fast and Funny Formula." More importantly, though, you can use the worksheet in writing your own sketches. Make photocopies first, and then use the copies for your actual writing.

WORKSHEET

Step 1 – Category:

Step 2 – Purpose:
    What's the point?

    Where's the joke?

Step 3 – Point of View/Frame of Reference:

Step 4 – Concept or Premise:

Step 5 – Outside Structure (4 Principles):

WORKSHEET *(continued)*

Step 6 – Inside Structure (Beats):

Step 7 – Filler (Dialogue and Action):

Step 8 – The Ending:

PART
FOUR

Beyond the Formula

Writing Alone Vs. Collaborating

Depending on your personal preference, you might choose to write alone, with a writing partner, or in collaboration with two or more people. Then again, you might do all of the above at different times for different projects. Whatever your choice, you'll find there are advantages and disadvantages to each method.

Writing alone will allow you maximum control over your ideas. Perhaps you've chosen an idea that's very personal, and you want to ensure that the piece has only one "voice" — yours. If you work singly, you won't run into conflicts about where the piece should go, who the characters should be, and what they should be saying, so the writing may go more quickly. And when you've struggled to bring a sketch to fruition and the sketch works, you won't have to share the sweet smell of success with anyone else!

Speaking for myself, I'm not completely comfortable relying on someone else in such a highly personal and creative endeavor as sketch writing. I've had people drop out of projects, or lose interest so that I had to pull them along (and then share the credit), or try to turn over the product to sources who weren't acceptable to me. Those are some of the potential pitfalls of working with others.

Let's say you decide to team up with another writer. Before you do, make certain it's someone who's trustworthy, has a similar degree of integrity, and whose talents complement your own. You don't necessarily need, or want, to collaborate with someone whose sense of humor is identical; in fact, the beauty of collaborating lies in the different "takes" each person brings to the idea or subject matter, thus expanding the creative possibilities. However, you do want to select someone with a compatible style of writing. Creating humor with another person is an intimate experience — a true marriage of the minds — and you'll want to grow together over time.

The biggest mistake I see writers make is choosing a partner without a thorough understanding of how that person writes. Perhaps they form a partnership after working together on only one sketch, or prior to checking out important characteristics like temperament, reliability, and the many other factors that should be assessed before going into business with someone. In this regard, writers are sometimes more idealistic and less practical than they need to be to protect themselves. And I've seen examples where writing partners go through a bitter breakup, and at some later time when one partner is in a position to sell a sketch they co-wrote, the sale comes to a complete halt because the former partners are still too angry to agree on the terms of the deal.

This brings me to an additional point: make certain the terms of your partnership are articulated in some type of contract, whether drafted by yourselves or an entertainment attorney (which I strongly suggest). With a contract, everyone is protected. So when creating a twosome, don't get caught up in the initial enthusiasm and laughter; take time to consider the more pragmatic aspects of partnership.

On the positive side of working with a partner, you'll have someone to bounce your ideas off of, to constantly encourage you and provide continuous support, to share the burden of making your sketch work, and with whom you can find fulfillment and friendship, camaraderie and stimulation. As the old adage goes: two minds are sometimes better than one. In addition, working with another can alleviate the sense of isolation and aloneness that often accompanies writing —

one of the loneliest occupations on earth. Again, it just depends on what works best for you.

To me, the hardest way to write is in collaboration with a team of people, but I know other writers who wouldn't think of cooking up comedy any other way. In my experience, there's a greater potential for divisiveness with more than two writers, including fights over what makes people laugh and the ideas to be used. Some sitcom writers working in teams complain that their creativity is diluted or goes unrecognized, and/or the process tends to bog down. (I've even witnessed a team of writers fight for several hours over one word in the script!) Sometimes, then, having more writers on board increases the potential for problems.

On the other hand, working with a group of creative people can be a lot of fun; and when the ideas start flying, they just seem to keep coming. In addition, a group of writers can often produce sketches of great depth and the added pizzazz that comes only from an ensemble effort. As a matter of fact, I recommend you write this way at least once; it can be a great experience. And as I mentioned, there are writers who insist that working with a team is the only way to make funny stuff truly great.

So there's no right or wrong in determining how you'll write; it's simply a matter of choice. Before you make a decision, though, be sure to make a list of the pros and cons according to your own preferences.

I tell my students my biggest goal for them is to learn to write alone, because I want them to be self-reliant. After all, you can always find a writing partner at some later point. Whatever happens, though, you'll always have yourself to fall back on under the best and worst of circumstances.

YOUR AUDIENCE VS. THE CRITICS

You've heard the expression "You can't please all of the people all of the time." That's certainly true in sketch comedy. Who should the writer of sketch comedy be aiming to please? If you're writing for a television show, you'd better please the producer. However, the majority of sketch comedy writers I know write for local theaters, small theaters in other towns, or for local comedy troupes, so they have other options.

If your work is being showcased at a live theater, you can tailor your work to suit yourself, your audiences, and/or the individual likes and dislikes of the critics reviewing your show. Naturally, you'd like to please all three factions. If that isn't possible, though, where should your focus be?

I must admit that for the first few years I was producing/ writing/directing sketch comedy shows, I was focused on reviewers' comments. During that time, I gained quite a bit of insight into what does and doesn't work on stage through helpful, constructive critiques by reviewers I respected. However, not all reviewers are worthy of respect; some are ruthless, inaccurate, mean-spirited individuals who clearly abuse their power. As I soon learned, it's not a good idea to tie your moods, sense of security, and confidence level to reviewers' opinions of your work — glowing or otherwise.

So if you're not going to focus your efforts on pleasing the critics, who should you be targeting? Well, I've concluded the opinions that really count are those of the audience. Instead of placing stock in how critics respond to my shows, I listen to the audience. I count on them to tell me and the actors what works and what doesn't.

(One cautionary note in this regard: be wary of the responses of family and friends, who are often biased in your favor. Instead, make your judgments based on neutral audiences composed of people you don't know.)

Over time, I've become keenly aware of audience responses, even the more subtle ones. I listen not only for laughs, but also to the different degrees of applause as the lights go out after each piece. Oftentimes, sketch work isn't written with constant laughter in mind; some pieces are quietly amusing, with simple pleasures or bits of satire that don't necessarily elicit laughs. However, when the sketch is over, the applause from audience members will indicate their level of appreciation.

I think there's total truth with an audience when it comes to comedy. Most people won't feign laughter; laughter and applause are impulsive acts. And if four or five consecutive audiences laugh or react at the same juncture in a sketch, then I know my writing instincts are correct. Audience reaction is my personal dipstick, if you will, for measuring my success as a writer. Always. As I tell my students, "What's the point of putting your work on stage if your aim and priority isn't the audience?"

This isn't to say, of course, that good reviews and enthusiastic audiences are mutually exclusive. It's not as though you have to choose between the two; the idea is to go for both. If you do decide to tailor your writing to the reactions of critics, be aware of that decision before you begin the sketch writing process. But take heed: I've seen many a critic give a bad review to a show that was really terrific. Conversely, critics will sometimes gush over a show that's less than worthy.

If you want to be regarded as a successful writer, you'll need to be able to pitch yourself with some credibility; and a portfolio of positive reviews is one way to do that. However, accolades from those who've seen your work are even more important. You never know when someone with the potential to advance your career might be in the audience — an agent, producer, someone who hires writing talent. In my own experience, I've been hired for sketch jobs more often on the basis of what someone's seen of my work rather than what someone's read about it.

One last piece of advice on this subject: always be true to yourself in your writing, but also be willing to subjugate your ego and listen to the people you're presenting your sketches to — audiences and/or critics. Standing on principle and pleasing only yourself can be a very lonely place to hang out.

◇16◇

HANdliNq REjECTiON

One of the most difficult aspects of being an artist of any kind is the constant vulnerability. After all, when your work is a very personal expression of your talent, rebuffs can be painful — both professionally and psychologically. Those in the high profile world of show business are especially strong candidates for rejection. For sketch comedy writers it can happen often, and even the best are not immune.

In my view, there are two major types of rejection. Type A occurs when your comedy fails to strike a responsive chord with the audience, and Type B when the person who's paying you for your work either doesn't like it, or has a completely different idea of how the piece should be written. Both types can occur at any point in your writing career; and even if you've developed a protective shield over time, rejection can still hurt.

On the other hand, I always maintain that in order to know success, you must occasionally fail. The experience of Type A rejection, in which your comedy piece elicits only a lackluster response from the audience, can teach you some very valuable lessons — lessons, I assure you, you won't soon forget, but which can increase your chances for success in the future.

Putting a sketch in front of an audience is the best way to get a clear picture of how the piece is firing. There have been times when something I thought was brilliantly clever bombed with my audience, and I cringed at the reaction; however, these were also the times that taught me the most about how to fix pieces to really make them work. (In fact, I soon learned to schedule preview nights for my shows, so I could make repairs *before* the critics arrived on opening night!)

Type A rejection, then, can actually stimulate mental activity and take you to new creative heights. In addition, it can help you to develop an inner sense of what does and doesn't work with an audience; and over the long term your confidence will build, because you'll be more likely to produce successful sketches. Hopefully, too, the experiences with negative audience reaction will serve to toughen you and build your resilience, so you'll learn not to take rejection personally. Remember: you aren't your work, and failure in sketch comedy is just like failure in anything else — just a small part of your overall being. And as one of my mentors once admonished me, if you're not making mistakes, you're not learning anything. So as painful as it may seem at the time, there's simply no substitute for the experience of Type A rejection.

Type B rejection, which comes from the client, can actually be more difficult for some writers to take, because it's a threat to both livelihood *and* self-esteem. (Just think: you can feel bad *and* face the prospect of being broke, all at the same time!) With Type B, you'll need to pay close attention to the needs of your client, whether it's the head writer for "*Saturday Night Live*" or the planner who's organizing a large industrial meeting or convention for a major corporation. Always remember: it's their show, and you want to consider them first. That doesn't automatically mean you'll have to compromise your creativity, voice, and edge; but you will need to direct your talents to building sketches that are appropriate in the eyes of your client. If you're good at what you do, you'll always make a project work — for both of you.

Versatility as a writer is a key element in adapting to the needs of individual clients. If you've had experience writing different types of copy — for example, advertising, journalism, publicity, sitcoms, brochures, etc. — you will have gained lots of practice in adjusting your writing style. And if you haven't had much writing experience, don't despair. Write within your range, then stretch and grow.

I've been fortunate to write for my own theater, as well as numerous large organizations and companies; and that has helped keep my writing style flexible and adaptable. For example, in preparing scripts for training programs offered by the State Bar of California, I was asked to revamp several of my initial concepts; and when I finally arrived at one my client liked, that script went through more than a dozen drafts before finally being approved. Rather than regard the changes as personal rejections, I saw them as minor corrections that were bringing me ever closer to meeting the needs of my client. Of course, I continued to argue points I felt strongly about — I always do — but the bigger picture involves retaining what you know works for the sketch, and compromising only in those places where your client insists on changes.

Remember: when you're getting paid to write, you must maintain an air of professionalism, which means you can't allow your feelings to interfere with getting the job done. If your work is rejected or requires modifications, be mature enough to note the suggestions, detach yourself a bit, and complete the job. Always work at finding a way to keep your sense of dignity and integrity intact, while at the same time meeting client demands — whether from a crusty television producer, an event planner, a live theater director, or the owner of a large corporation. If you can maintain this perspective, you'll be able to weather Type B rejection as successfully as Type A, and even to learn from it.

If you're experiencing another type of rejection altogether — that is, none of your work is being accepted, whether submitted for pay or free of charge — then you'll want to continue to study and fine-tune your skills. Perseverance and diligence are key here.

Alternatively, if you've had some success but have recently encountered a series of turndowns, I'd recommend that you regroup and collect yourself by taking a short vacation from writing. Sometimes the best thing you can do for yourself is to turn off your computer and go out for an ice cream. Indulge and pamper yourself in some way that's meaningful to you. Then, when you return to your work, you can analyze it from a fresh perspective and restart the writing process. (Incidentally, this is one of those times when having a writing partner or two is a big help: you can support and console one another through the rough spots.)

To recap a very important point from this chapter: rejection is a fact of life in show business. Don't take it personally, and never allow it to compromise your self- esteem, your sense of well-being, your dreams. Detach yourself to some extent in order to maintain a healthy perspective and to keep moving forward with your writing. Surprisingly, the most insecure writers I've encountered are the ones who've never experienced significant failures with their sketches: they're uncertain whether any of their stuff ever *really* worked. So take heed: rejection — Type A, B, whatever — can actually be good for you!

Maintaining Your Sense of Humor and Source of Inspiration

Let's say you do encounter rejection along the way in your writing career — a fairly likely prospect. When that happens, you'll need to know how to retain your sense of humor (the cornerstone of your work!) and how to replenish your reservoir of inspiration.

With regard to maintaining your sense of humor, it'll be a lot easier if you heed my earlier advice: Don't take rejection personally. I've known many writers who became intimidated and/or dejected in the face of "No, thank you" responses from others; and yes, it's hard to feel humorous when you think your work isn't worthy. However, you simply can't allow lack of acceptance to break your spirit. Always remember the two absolute prerequisites to becoming a successful sketch comedy writer: perseverance and diligence. So, again, never let rejection get you down!

Another way to hold on to your sense of humor is to force yourself to write every single day, no matter what. If you can discipline yourself to write on bad days as well as good, you're on your way to becoming a consummate professional. What you'll discover with a daily regimen is your sense of humor is an entity unto itself, one that's always present and can't be diminished or eradicated by outside circumstances.

Writing on a daily basis is a way of exercising and toning your humor muscle. The more you use it, the stronger it'll become. And I can't tell you what a boost that will be to your confidence level. Granted, there will always be days when the humor comes more easily than others; but I know many great writers who can go to the notepad or computer keyboard and bang out a sketch, no matter what's taking place in their lives.

Sometimes, in fact, writing about your wounded ego, your feelings of rejection, or things that are irritating and frustrating — at that moment in time — can be a great source for some very special comedy skits. So, even if you're depressed and feel like crawling into something (I've always opted for my clothes hamper — I'm small), snap out of it! Force yourself to write. Writing in the face of everyday disasters is a terrific way to sharpen and extend your base of humor, and to demonstrate to yourself that you can write your way around life's obstacles, or even better, make humorous use of them.

Some of you are probably thinking: "But I can only write in spurts." Well, that's okay. Many writers fall into this category; and sketch comedy writing itself is often seasonal work. I know there've been periods when I've written every day for three months and then taken a two-month break. However, I think you'll notice the more you write, the easier it'll be to get that initial momentum going, and the more your writing will flow. Soon you'll begin to create almost automatically — perhaps a subconscious response to sitting down in front of the computer. So, one way to retain your sense of humor is simply to keep using it in your ongoing writing routine.

Just a note here: It took me several years working as a copywriter to prove to myself I could tackle assignments without the crushing anxiety of going to the keyboard and wondering if I'd be able to fill up that blank screen. But like I said, the more you write, the easier it becomes. And in my view, the truly professional writers are the ones who can write every day of the year, despite whatever else is going on in terms of rejection, distractions, or general lack of interest.

Now, if you're feeling down, one way to stimulate your

sense of humor is to turn to a favorite funny book or movie, or call a friend who shares your particular view of what's humorous. (I often call my sister in these instances, because we have a rich history of silliness from our years of growing up together!) Since laughter tends to neutralize negative feelings and provide a fresh perspective on things, these various sources will have you back on track in no time. In addition, they'll serve as a constant reminder that your sense of humor is unflappable.

An additional method for toning your humor muscle is to do things that cause you to laugh at yourself. For example, one of my writing students makes a point of throwing a childish tantrum whenever one of his comedy pieces is rejected. After a few minutes, he feels so foolish that he starts laughing. Another student told me he once wore a shower curtain — rings and all — to a football game; and when people burst out laughing at the sight of him, he felt uplifted. That was his way of reassuring himself he was still funny.

The point is, whatever pulls you from the depths of despair and makes you laugh is what you want to be doing. Humor reorients you, like pushing the reset button. Besides, if you take things too seriously, you're more likely to ride the writer's roller coaster; and soon there'll be only certain select, peak times when you're able to write. Quite frankly, that's frighteningly limiting.

One final suggestion for keeping a firm grip on your sense of humor: Take a time-out when needed. Sometimes a day or two away from writing will provide a readjustment, a recharging of your mental battery; and with renewed energy, you're more likely to generate good sketch ideas — and perhaps even propel yourself to a whole new level of humor.

My advice to you is to find whatever it is that keeps you from disconnecting from your sense of humor, or abandoning it altogether. Remember: Your sense of humor is like the tip of your nose; it's always there, even though you may not be focused on it. And although you may temporarily abandon your sense of humor, it won't abandon you. If you need a vacation from it in order to regroup, just realize it'll always be available when you're ready to tap back into it. I, myself, check on my sense of humor every day, just to make sure it's still there. How? I do something to make myself — or someone else — laugh. Simple stuff like that.

To recap this section of the chapter: You can pull yourself out of a downward spiral by finding ways to stay light and humorous. It's in periods of lightness that your sense of humor will tend to prevail, coloring your overall mental picture and life experiences. And as a comedy writer, you'll need to constantly observe the world around you in order to activate your humor muscle — the core of your comedy writing.

Now, with regard to the second major topic of this chapter — how to preserve or renew your source of inspiration — I have a number of suggestions. For one, you can keep returning to the things that anchor you, whether it's a famous pearl of wisdom you've taped to your briefcase, a daily telephone call to your mother, a church service, or a passage from a favorite self-help book.

Most of us have sayings, mantras, or reminders that lift our psyches and center us. For myself, there's a famous quote from Winston Churchill that I keep nearby. It reads, "The definition of power is the ability to go from failure to failure with enthusiasm." Additionally, I have a bumper sticker that advises "Don't take life so seriously; it's only a temporary situation"; and a pair of tap shoes I inherited when my mother passed away that I slip into on an as-needed basis. They're a constant reminder that she's still with me, cheering me on.

The above recommendations are made for people in need of inspiration because they're feeling down, discouraged, disappointed, rejected, insecure, or in need of a boost, and so on. However, there are other reasons for seeking sources of inspiration, including the desire to remain motivated enough to continue writing — certainly a Herculean task when the writing effort exceeds the writing payoff.

As a writer, there will probably be times when you don't feel up to the job; or you've temporarily forgotten why you're writing in the first place; or you've written so steadily that you've run out of ideas to pull from. At these critical points in your writing career, you're more likely to stay motivated if you have a reliable source of inspiration — an "inspirational well," if you will, that you can dip into whenever your enthusiasm needs restoring.

When I teach writing classes, one of the first assignments I give my students is to make a list of what inspires them to keep going even when they don't feel like it; what, in particular, spurs them to go on creating sketches despite numerous attempts that simply don't come together; and what gets them back on their feet after their work is rejected. The reason for this assignment? They're going to need this collection of lists to return to from time to time for a quick jolt of inspiration, a fresh perspective, and reminders that'll keep them on course.

I know many writers who simply get bored with the writing process and need to rekindle their creative spark by seeking new fodder for their comedy material. Writers in this group might gain inspiration from reading newspapers, people watching, revisiting their lists of comedy ideas, and generally trying to tap into the initial passion that led them down the sketch writing trail in the first place.

My ultimate suggestion for maintaining your sense of humor and/or your source of inspiration is to direct yourself to your early years. Look there for what consistently made you laugh, or for recollections that give you a sense of your own courage, bravery, and ability to persevere in the face of difficulties. Remember: if you decide to stick with sketch comedy writing over the long haul, your sense of humor and sources of inspiration will be the survival tools of choice.

◈18◈

How to Package and Sell Your Sketch Comedy

The entertainment industry is extremely competitive, and making money as a comedy writer is just as difficult as making money in any other aspect of that profession. As with actors, there are more talented writers than there are available jobs. So in order to succeed, you'll need both talent and tenacity. In addition, you'll want to examine your reasons for writing sketch comedy. Are you doing it only for fun, or are you also hoping to make money at it? If it's the latter, you'll need to learn how to appropriately package and sell your comedy material.

The first thing to be aware of is that you should always present yourself and your work in a professional manner. In terms of your scripts, that means all materials should be typewritten, free of typos, and in a format that adheres to industry guidelines. Additionally, dialogue should be easy to read, and stage directions, set descriptions, and explanations of action should be clear and succinct. Keep in mind that the reader is seeing your piece for the first time, so the explanatory details must be sharp and easy to visualize. (For examples of what I'm talking about, please turn to the sample sketches in the "Sketches That Work" chapter.)

When submitting a script — whether to a local comedy troupe for a nonpaying gig, to an agent (if seeking representation), or to anyone else in the industry — be careful not to overwhelm them with too many samples of your work. Two or three of your favorite sketches are sufficient to give them a feel for your comedic voice and level of expertise; and if they want to see more, they'll ask. In addition, you'll want to send along a short, well-written cover letter that includes your address, telephone number, and any other pertinent information, and also a short bio and/or brief resume of your writing credits, if you have any. But please remember, you're sending your material to people who pore over scripts all day long; they're unlikely to spend time sorting through written debris to extract the pertinent facts. In sum, be sure to keep all your materials short and to the point.

Before you submit any material, make absolutely certain your pieces are protected by copyrights or pending copyrights. Most television shows and large comedy organizations won't even look at your material unless it comes to them through an agent or lawyer. In some cases you'll be asked to sign certain release forms, to prevent you from later alleging that your ideas were stolen by the show or organization, and then attempting to sue them.

If you don't have an agent and are planning to submit your work to a television executive or the producer of a network show, I strongly suggest you do it through an entertainment lawyer. There are a number of attorneys who will make submissions on your behalf at reasonable rates, or make agreements to the effect that they'll get paid if you are signed. Practically speaking, the attorney stands to make a good deal of money off you if you're hired, because he or she will most likely be the one who negotiates your subsequent writing contract.

An alternative approach is to find agent representation. There's a wonderful resource book called *The Working Actor's Guide*, available at all major bookstores. It offers listings of every reputable agent in the business, including agents who specialize in representing writers. You can call such agencies, find out which ones are accepting new clients, and then send them your material. One note: It's easier to be considered as a client if you know someone who can recommend you to the agent; cold submissions are much tougher. In this very competitive business, it *IS* who you know that counts; so if you have contacts, be sure to use them. You can always return the favor one day when you're successful!

If you're fortunate enough to elicit interest in your work prior to getting representation, make sure your financial compensation is commensurate with that of other writers of comparable experience. And quickly thereafter find impartial representation to ensure your interests are well protected from that point forward.

Whatever method you choose for putting yourself out there in the marketplace — alone or through an agent or lawyer — remember that getting placed or making the sale takes drive and perseverance. I don't know many writers who are "overnight" successes. Most of them have written for free for various improv/sketch groups at one time or another, pounded on doors, submitted and then resubmitted their pieces, and revised numerous drafts of the same pieces before arriving at some that worked. Yes, writers are big dues payers! Again, I can't stress enough the importance of a strong will and dogged determination in achieving comedy writing success.

I've discussed what to do if you're trying to package and sell your product to the entertainment industry. What about other possible sources, though? There are many ways to make money as a sketch writer. For example, some sketch and comedy groups pay their writers. Granted, the sum isn't large, but they do pay something. And that can be a great start for people who are still honing their skills and finding out what works and what doesn't.

At the other extreme, one of the most lucrative markets for sketch writers is the corporate world. Such jobs are known in the trade as "industrials." Major event planning organizations, video companies, trade show coordinators, training companies, and a variety of others hire writers to prepare the comedic segments of their yearly conventions, annual meetings, motivational seminars, training workshops, and so on. Tracking down these organizations takes some work, but one shortcut is to contact various hotels and large meeting facilities, such as convention centers, and ask who's staging events that call for comedy entertainment. Many organizations and companies are eagerly searching out people with sketch writing talent.

In addition, there are a number of companies looking for writers to provide sketches and skits as a way of putting their public service or training messages across. I do a great deal of work along these lines, and I truly love it. For one such assignment, I was hired to write and create on behalf of The Tobacco Youth Prevention Program. So not only did I have the opportunity to showcase my humor and creativity, but I was also part of a meaningful crusade to help youngsters. As a result, the work was doubly gratifying.

If you're considering a sketch writing career in the peripheral entertainment field of industrials, be assured that it's possible to make a very good living at it. After all, not everyone needs to write for *"Saturday Night Live"* or some other high-profile television show. The same rules apply, though, so make certain you present yourself and your work in a very professional way.

One final note: Develop a good record-keeping system from the outset, and make it a policy to keep organized files of your scripts, submissions, and clients. If you can obtain videotapes of your work, keep a library of them as well. Additionally, you'll want to have files for idea logs, character profiles, scripts you may want to finish one day, and so on. In general, make sure all your materials are organized and easily accessible, because you never know when you'll need to retrieve something for reference or a quick submission to someone important. There's nothing worse than writers who are too scattered to get their hands on leads, names of agents and producers, completed scripts, tapes, etc. So, in closing, stay organized!

EPILOGUE

Now that you're nearly at the end of this book, I hope you've gained a lot of valuable information along the way on the design, construction, and refinement of your sketch comedy pieces, and what to do with your sketches once you've created them. With the "Fast and Funny Formula" as your starting point, you're well on your way to becoming a sketch comedy writer. Although being a writer isn't an easy life, I can tell you from firsthand experience that it's often a very rewarding one. To me, there's nothing more gratifying than having your comedy piece come to life on stage exactly as you envisioned it — or sometimes even exceeding your expectations — and at the same time having an audience respond enthusiastically to what you've created. It's the ultimate thrill!

And while it's true that sketch comedy writing can be a difficult skill to master, it's equally true that — like anything else — with enough time and practice, it will gradually become a more natural and joyful process. As you repeatedly engage in the process of writing, somewhere along the way you'll discover that you've accumulated an abundance of confidence. (There's something about revising something again and again until it works that really boosts your confidence level!) Eventually you'll find yourself producing funnier pieces at a much faster pace, incorporating all those wonderful ideas you've been carrying around, until finally you'll discover that you've crossed over from working toward your potential to fully realizing it.

It's been my goal with this book to send you out into the sketch writing world armed with the tools and guidelines you'll need to construct comedy pieces that will consistently work with your audiences. So, then, if you haven't done so already, it's time to pull out your "Fast and Funny Formula" worksheet, along with that log of humorous ideas you've been collecting, and to carefully work through the eight steps of the formula. If you do, I'm confident you will, in a very solid way, "Build To Laugh."

ABOUT THE AUTHOR

A founding member of the world-famous L.A. Groundlings, Cherie Kerr was the founder in 1990 and the Executive Producer and Artistic Director for the Orange County Crazies, a sketch and improvisational comedy troupe in Santa Ana, California. She also served as the group's head writer. She has received rave reviews for her work as a writer, performer and director.

Kerr has taught improvisational comedy to actors for the past 30 years, and teaches other classes as well, including a class on how to develop original characters and how to write sketch comedy. She has studied with some of the best improve and comedy teachers in the business, including Gary Austin, founder of the L.A. Groundlings, and a former member of the highly acclaimed group, The Committee; Michael Gellman, a director and teacher for Second City, in Chicago; and Jeannie Berlin (an Academy Award nominee and Elaine May's daughter.) In her formative years, she studied at the Pasadena Academy of Drama with Eleanor Dopp.

A writer for more than 30 years, Kerr has owned an award-winning public relations firm and still works as a consultant in that field. She has written, produced and directed an original full-scale musical comedy, is a member of ASCAP, and has been honored as an award-winning journalist and publicist. Kerr was named, along with Disney's Michael Eisner, as one of the "Top Ten Most Sensational People in Orange County," by *Orange Coast Magazine.* She has been quoted in many publications including the *OC Register, New York Times, Los Angeles Times, Miami Herald, Harvard Review Communication Newsletter, Forbes, American Way* magazine, *Sacramento Bee, Investor's Business Daily* and Associated Press, in addition to many others.

Kerr also starred in her own one-woman show, *Out of Her Mind,* which was met with great success and which she single-handedly wrote. In it she played a number of original characters.

Cherie Kerr founded ExecuProv in 1983 and has provided a variety of classes on presentation and communication skills to hundreds of business professionals. Her clients include Ericcson, Toyota, Kawasaki, Mitsubishi, Ingram Micro, Bank One, Delta Dental, Experian, Foothill Capital, PacifiCare, Allergan, Universal Studios, Fluor Corporation, 3i Implant, ConAgra Goods, The Hilton Hotel and Marriot Hotel Corporations, California Trucking Association, Office Max/Boise, Office Depot and the U.S. Naval Academy at Annapolis, to name a few. She also has worked for a number of governmental agencies including the L.A. City Attorney's Office, the L.A. District Attorney's office, the County of Orange, the Orange County Bar Foundation and the Orange County Juvenile Drug Court Program. She is a certified Provider for the Continuing Legal Education Program for the State Bar of California, and has served as that organization's official speaker-trainer for its Board of Governors.

In addition to lecturing and teaching ExecuProv

courses, both in classroom situations and in private, one-on-one coaching sessions, Kerr provides speechwriting services for many of her clients. Kerr also provides her creative services to large companies for corporate comedy industrials and also offers Public Relations consultant services through her award-winning PR firm, Kerr PR.

Kerr is frequently sought out as a keynote speaker addressing presentation and communication skills and humor in the workplace.

In addition to *Build to Laugh: How to Construct Sketch Comedy with the Fast and Funny Formula*, Kerr has also written *The Bliss or "Diss" Connection? Email Etiquette For The Business Professional; Funny Business: How To Make You Laugh On The Job Every Day; How To Think Fast On Your Feet (Without Putting Them In Your Mouth); Death by PowerPoint: How To Avoid Killing Your Presentation and Sucking the Life Out of Your Audience; "When I Say This...," "Do You Mean That?"*, a book addressing one-on-one communication on the job; and a book on public speaking skills, *"I've Asked Miller To Say A Few Words"*, as well as a book on how to get humor and good storytelling into speeches and presentations, *"What's So Funny?"*. All of her books use improv comedy techniques as the basis for the lessons. She has also penned her first major literary work, *Charlie's Notes, A Memoir*, the story of her father's life as a jazz musician.

Cherie Kerr resides in Santa Ana, California. She is the mother of three and also has four grandchildren.

ExecuProv offers workshop sessions, seminars and private coaching to both companies and individuals worldwide. Ms. Kerr is available for keynote speeches and special appearances. Please submit a written request for any of the above to:

ExecuProv
DePietro Performance Center
809 N. Main Street
Santa Ana, CA 92701

Email: CherieKerr@aol.com
Visit ExecuProv's website: www.ExecuProv.com

Other Books By Cherie Kerr

The Bliss or "Diss" Connection?
Email Etiquette For The Business Professional

Funny Business:
How To Make <u>You</u> Laugh On The Job Every Day

"I've Asked Miller to Say a Few Words" *—New and Exciting*
Ways to Improve Speaking and Presentation Skills Through the Use
of Improvisational Comedy Techniques
Foreword by Phil Hartman

"What's So Funny?" *—How to Get Good Storytelling and*
Humor Into Your Speeches and Presentations

"When I Say This…," ***"Do You Mean That?"*** *— Enhancing*
On-The-Job Communications Skills Using the Rules and Tools of
The Improv Comedy Player
Foreword by Julia Sweeney

How To Think Fast On Your Feet (Without Putting Them In
Your Mouth)
For The Business Professional Who Doesn't
Know What To Say When…

Death By PowerPoint:
How To Avoid Killing Your Presentation
and Sucking the Life Out of Your Audience

Charlie's Notes: A Memoir

Coming Soon

Wit's End: *How To Deal With Difficult People*

I would like to order the following books:

_____

_____

_____

Name _____

Address _____

City _____

State _____ Zip _____

Telephone No. _____ Fax No. _____

Email Address_____

Credit Card _____ Visa _____ MasterCard

Credit Card No. _____

Expiration Date _____

Signature _____

_____ Please put me on your email list to be informed of upcoming classes held at the DePietro Performance Center.

Please Mail order forms to :

ExecuProv Press
DePietro Performance Center
809 N. Main Street
Santa Ana, CA 92701

Kerr's books are also available at Amazon.com, Barnes&Noble.com and at all major bookstores throughout the country.

focus on what's going on now — not future or past

start w/ "I" or "You"

don't talk about people off stage

let your emotional state affect your action (angry → move faster, etc)

---

est. relationship

be affected by the scene

Characters — mostly play yourself

realism over over acting

don't be overtly clowny.